DATE

miles

N

0

R. Slaney

Atlantic Ocean

L E I N S T E R

Enniskerry
Rathdrum
Avoca
Arklow
WICKLOW
WICKLOW MTNS.
Lugnaquillia ▲
Nass
KILDARE
Mt. Leinster ▲
WEXFORD
Wexford
Carlow
CARLOW
Clonmacnoise
Kilkenny
New Ross
LAOIGHIS
KILKENNY
Slievenamon ▲
Clonmel
Waterford
Dungarvan
Helvick Head
WATERFORD
Ardmore
Cashel
Lismore
Youghal
TIPPERARY
Lough Derg
GALWAY
Limerick
Galway Bay
CLARE
Sixmilebridge
Shannon
Adare
LIMERICK
R. Shannon
M U N S T E R
CORK
Cork
Blarney
Kinsale
Slieve Elva
Lisdoonvarna
Ardfert
Tralee
KERRY
Mt. Brandon ▲
DINGLE PENINSULA
Dingle
Dingle Bay
Killorglin
Lough Leane
Cahirciveen
Kenmare
Kenmare River
Glengarriff
Castletownbere
Bantry Bay
Skellig Rocks

© 1997, Mark Stein Studios

Tommy Makem's
SECRET IRELAND

Tommy Makem's

SECRET IRELAND

Tommy Makem

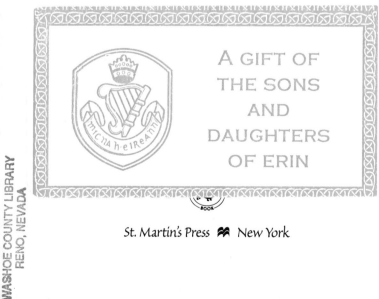

A GIFT OF
THE SONS
AND
DAUGHTERS
OF ERIN

St. Martin's Press 🕮 New York

A THOMAS DUNNE BOOK.
An Imprint of St. Martin's Press.

Endpaper map © 1997, Mark Stein Studios

Production Editor: David Stanford Burr

Design: Nancy Resnick

Library of Congress Cataloging-in-Publication Data

Makem, Tommy.
    Tommy Makem's Secret Ireland / Tommy Makem. — 1st ed.
        p.   cm.
    ISBN 0-312-15675-8
    1. Ireland—Description and travel.   2. Makem, Tommy—Homes
and haunts—Ireland.   3. Folk songs, English—Ireland—Texts.
4. Folk singers—Ireland—Biography. 5. Historic sites—Ireland.
6. Ireland—Civilization. I. Title.
DA978.2.M34   1997
941.5—dc21   97-7601
                                              CIP

First Edition: May 1997

10 9 8 7 6 5 4 3 2 1

For my wife Mary,
Katie, Shane, Conor, Rory and Molly—
for all their support

Contents

INTRODUCTION

Ireland

A shimmering emerald eye
Piercing the blue Atlantean sweep,
Ever looking westward
To the great Bower of Sol.
A beacon; a seductive siren;
A rock of time.
Luscious; verdant; fertile;
Coursed by the three great waves,
Cliodna, Ruari, and Toth.
Land for poets; land for heroes;
A Dagda's Cauldron of light.
This Banba; This Fodhla; This Eriu;
Eternal, many splendoured Ireland.

—TOMMY MAKEM

The land sings a very ancient song. Its highways and byways run quietly through beautiful, ever-changing country scenes. Important places and monuments surprise the traveller around almost every bend of the road. The people are warm and welcoming, their character shaped and moulded through the millennia by a motley line of ancestors.

According to Eleanor Hull in her wonderful book *Pagan Ireland,* Noah had a granddaughter named Cessair. When he was building the ark, Cessair asked Noah to keep a place for her father, herself and her husband on it. Noah said that he did not have room for them and he advised them to go to the western part of the world where no one yet lived and sin had not been committed. Cessair was very angered by this and said that she and her people would forsake Noah's god and worship instead, an idol they had with them. So Cessair with her husband Fintan, her father, her brother and fifty maidens set out for the western part of the world. According to the *Annals of the Four Masters* they landed in Ireland forty days before the Flood began. The Flood eventually overtook them there and all were drowned except Fintan who survived in various forms to tell the tales of all the races who subsequently inhabited Ireland.

Before the five invasions chronicled in the *Book of Invasions,* the people who built the Newgrange complex and other ancient sites, seem to have inhabited Ireland somewhere between 3000 and 4000 B.C.

The Parthalonians arrived in Ireland about 2035 B.C. They are said to have come from Scythia in southwestern Europe and adjoining portions of Asia. Parthalon and his followers lived chiefly between Tallaght and Howth in County Dublin. That district was known as Magh nEalta (The Plain of the Bird Flocks). Parthalon himself only lived for thirty years after his arrival in Ireland, but his followers and descendants inhabited Ireland for nearly three hundred years. They were eventually wiped out by a terrible plague.

The name Tallaght or Tamlacht, where they are said to be buried, means "Plague Grave." On the hill, graves and burial mounds have been found that contained cinerary urns.

Nemedius and his sons led one thousand colonists from the shores of the Euxine Sea, now known as the Black Sea, to Ireland where they landed around 1727 B.C. They were harrassed by fleets of Fomorian pirates, who were thought to have come from Africa, but Eleanor Hull contends it is more likely that they came from northern Europe. The Nemedians defeated the Fomorians in three battles but more and more pirates kept arriving and they eventually enslaved the Nemedians. The Fomorians imposed a heavy tribute on the Nemedians. Every year at Samhain (Halloween) they had to give two thirds of their children, their corn and their milk cows, besides flour, cream and butter in abundance. This tax was collected by a female steward called Liagh.

The Nemedians became so angered with paying this tax that they banded together and attacked and destroyed the Fomorian tower and stronghold on Tory Island, off the coast of County Donegal. Fresh companies of robbers kept arriving and the Nemedians decided to leave the country. They scattered in different directions leaving only a small remnant behind.

One of the Nemedian chiefs who left Ireland at that time was called Simeon Breac, the son of Starn. He and his followers went to Greece. Simeon Breac and his followers became so numerous that the Greeks enslaved them out of terror of their increasing power. Part of their slave duty was to carry leather bags of rich soil from the fertile valleys up to the stony hills in order to turn them into gardens. Because of this work they became known as Firbolgs or "men of the bags." Unable to stand their slavery, they either made boats out of their leather bags or stole boats from their Greek masters and escaped. The Firbolgs returned to Ireland in 1470 B.C., 217 years after their ancestor Simeon Breac had flown from it.

The Firbolgs did not bear a very good name in Ireland, but this is the opinion of their enemies. Many proofs indicate that this opinion was invalid. For instance, Ferdia, the great friend and eventual opponent of Cuchullain was as skilled and as great a warrior, as brave and noble as he, and Ferdia was a Firbolg. During *An Tain Bo Culaigne* (The Cattle Raid of Cooley), Ireland's greatest mythological epic, the Firbolg, who were part of the army of Leinster, were noted for their quickness and cleverness. They reputedly had set up camp and lighted their fires before the rest of the army had even reached the camping ground.

In 1400 B.C. the magical Tuatha De Danaan (People of the goddess Dana) made their first appearance in Cong in County Mayo. They were highly cultured, capable, skilled in arts and crafts and possessed of many magical powers. The Firbolgs came to refer to them as necromancers. In later times they were looked upon as great gods, the deities of the pagan Irish. From the Otherworld, they brought to Ireland knowledge of medicine, of building, of making cups and weapons from brass and other metals; besides the skill in harp playing for which the Irish afterwards became so famous.

The Tuatha De Danaan defeated the Firbolg in a four-day battle on the Plain of South Moytura, near Cong. It was known as the First Battle of Moytura. The Firbolg king Eochaid was killed on the last day of the battle.

After their defeat, the Firbolg who escaped, fled to the western isles of Arran, Rathlin and the Hebrides. Some of them later returned to Ireland and settled mostly in Connaught, but with a few in Leinster.

In the Second Battle of Moytura, fought some twenty-seven years later in North Moytura, near Sligo, the Tuatha De Danaan defeated the Fomorians. The Fomorian king, Balor of the Evil Eye was killed by his grandson Lugh of the Long Hand, who was half Fomorian and half De Danaan, during the battle. King Nuada of the Silver Hand, the De Danaan king, was also killed in that battle by the Fomorian champion Sreng. The Dagda Mor, considered the greatest of the De Danaan gods, succeeded Nuada as king.

The Milesians, who arrived in Ireland around 1100 B.C., came from Scythia by way of Egypt, Crete and Spain. One of their prophets foretold that they would inhabit Inisfail (The Island of Destiny). They landed with thirty ships at Inver Slainge, the mouth of the River Slaney in Wexford harbour. The De Danaans raised a great mist so they couldn't find the shore. They put to sea again and sailed around the south coast until they reached County Kerry. Again the De Danaan raised a thick mist and they had great difficulty in landing. Eventually they did land and set off to meet the De Danaan leaders at Tara. Amergin, the Milesian bard challenged the De Danaan to battle, but the De Danaan princes refused. A compromise was reached with the Milesians to return to Kerry and put to sea again at Inver Sceine (the River Kenmare, named Sceine for Amergin's wife who died there). The Milesians were to sail out to a distance of nine waves from the shore and if the De Danaans could once more prevent them from landing, they were to leave Ireland. If the Milesians succeeded, the De Danaan had to go. The De Danaans, by magic, raised a tremendous storm against them. Most of their ships were wrecked and many were killed including five of the sons of Mil. One of them, Donn, and all his crew were lost at what has been called in the old stories, "The House of Donn." Ir, another brother, was thrown up on the rocks of Skellig Michael. Only three of Mil's sons survived; Eber, Eremon and Amergin. Amergin the bard divided up the country, allowing the De Danaan to occupy all under the earth where they established their raths and forts. According to some they are still there and we have come to know them as the leprechauns and the sidhe (pronounced shee). Eber was given the southern half of Ireland and Eremon, the northern half. Amergin, being a bard, did not need any property. Eber's wife, not being content with what she had, wanted the "loveliest hill in Ireland," Tara, which was in Eremon's half. She set her husband to war against his brother and Eber was killed. So, she lost everything as Eremon became ruler of the whole country.

In more recent times, the Vikings, the Normans and the Anglo-Saxons came. Along with some changes brought by Christianity in the fifth century A.D., the contributions of all these ancient peoples have left Ireland a magical, mythical place.

In That Land

Come with me and I'll take you to the land of my
    fathers,
Where wild heather mountains look out to the sea.
You will find hearts as kind as the soft winds of
    summer,
And a warm welcome waiting for you and for me.

Chorus:
In that land, of song and story,
In that land, where legends dwell,
In that land, enshrined in glory,
In that land, that land I love so well.

Let your feet walk the green hills where the heroes
    have battled
For freedom and honour and glory and right;
Where the birds sing the praises of men who were
    gallant,
The first in the fray and the last to take flight.

Chorus:

You can walk the bright meadows when the flow-
    ers are all blooming,

Or fish the deep waters, forgetting all your care,
You can sing with the lark as she welcomes the
    morning,
Or hunt for the pheasant, the fox, and the hare.

Chorus:

If your bones they are weary and your mind is un-
    easy,
The troubles of life, they are taking their toll,
Come with me to a green land of laughter and leg-
    end,
There's rest for the body and peace for the soul.

Chorus:

—TOMMY MAKEM

1

WHERE BOAND'S RIVER FLOWS

Slane

Let us not begin our journey in modern Ireland, but rather in the ancient heart of this storied land. We leave behind the fair city of Dublin and make our way northward through Finglas of the Fair Rill and what Ledwidge, the poet called "White Ashbourne." After twenty or so miles of pleasant travelling by long, straight roads, we turn a bend in the road and down below us is the legendary River Boyne. As we cross the bridge with the strangely angled waterfall on our left, we see Slane Castle, the home of Lord Mountcharles peeping through the trees. Climbing the hill on the other side of the bridge, the village of Slane in County Meath suddenly appears.

Here at this crossroads, we can see four identical houses, one on each corner. They are said to have been built by a local landowner for his four daughters, so that all four would feel equal.

The road to the left takes us to the town of Navan and on to the Hill of Tara. Straight ahead to the north is the Hill of Slane.

We are taking the road to the right, out of Slane. This road runs on to Oldbridge and Drogheda. A mile or so out this road is the home of the poet, Francis Ledwidge, who was killed in Flanders during the Great War in 1917.

Travelling past Ledwidge's cottage, we take a road to the right and eventually approach our first destination, Newgrange, or Brugh Na Boinne as it is called in Irish. Brugh Na Boinne means the Palace of the Boyne, and Brugh also means the whole area, or complex. It is a most impressive sight, having been restored to great splendour and has an atmosphere that never fails to leave me awestruck.

A detail of one of the six hundred decorated megalithic stones that are to be found in the Newgrange complex. (photo provided by Irish Tourist Board)

Newgrange

Newgrange, popularly known as a megalithic gravesite, is between five and six thousand years old, dating from the fourth millennium B.C. Reputed to be the oldest man-made building in the world, it outdates the Egyptian pyramids and outdates Stonehenge by at least a thousand years and perhaps as much as fifteen hundred years.

The site covers an acre and the building is circular, with a three-hundred-foot diameter. The front of the building is faced with white quartz from the Wicklow Mountains, some fifty miles to the south. It also has inserts of round shaped granite stones from the Mourne Mountains, fifty miles to the north. The popular theory is that both the quartz from Wicklow and the granite from Mourne were brought here by some form of raft along the seacoast from both directions, and then up the River Boyne to Newgrange.

There are twelve standing stones a short distance out from the building, but there are only theories as to where they originated. Previously, there were thirty-five, and they were thought to be a boundary "for the dreaded spirits of the dead, so that they should not transgress it and molest the living."

Brugh Na Boinne

Where Boand's river twists and turns and flows,
And Brugh Na Boinne lights up the shining hill;
In winter's deepest darkness no light glows
To warm the earth, or ease death's bitter chill.
But on the shortest day the sun returns,
Renewing life and hope in earth and bones,
He climbs the Brugh's dark passage, where he burns;
His message carved on rows of standing stones.
And here I stand beside the entrance stone,
With all the years of darkness nearly done;
I feel the voices singing in my bone,
The ancient pulsing of the moon and sun.
And hidden knowledge, by some mystic power
Has been refound, to light man's shining hour.

—Tommy Makem

There are ninety-seven kerbstones around the building, a number of them with carvings, but the most elaborate and best known of all the carved stones in the complex, is undoubtedly the entrance stone at the doorway to the chamber. This stone is regarded as the finest example of megalithic art in the world.

The passage climbing into the cruciform shaped chamber is 62 feet long and is lined on both sides by 43 orthostats, or upright stones, many of them decorated. These orthostats vary in height from 5 to 8 feet and when Newgrange was excavated, it was deduced that the carvings must have been done before the stones were set up in place.

The cruciform chamber is made up of a central chamber with a 20-foot high corbelled roof and three smaller chambers opening off of it. Each of the three smaller chambers has a stone basin, presumably used to hold the ashes of the cremated dead. Some of the stones forming the corbelled roof of the central chamber had grooves cut into them to direct whatever water might seep through the cairn away from the chamber. No water has run into it for over five thousand years!

The Beaker People, as the people who built the edifice were known, were not only clever engineers and architects, but also very skilled in astronomy. There is an opening over the entrance to the chamber called, in recent times, a window box. It faces east and is so precisely placed that during the winter solstice (19–23 December), the shortest days in the year, the sun shines through the window box and climbs up the passage between the orthostats. It shines on the back wall and illuminates the chamber for about seventeen minutes.

The ancient peoples believed that their sun god, the giver of light, heat and all life, had been off fighting the forces of darkness through the darkest time of the year and on returning in victory penetrated mother earth, renewing life and hope in everything in the earth, on the earth and over the earth. They knew the course of the sun, the moon and the planets and could plan their lives in accordance with celestial courses and movements.

There are two other mounds that form part of the Newgrange complex: Dowth, about a mile or so to the east of Newgrange, which has not yet been excavated, and Knowth, about a mile or so west of Newgrange, which has been excavated and contains a great wealth of large carved stones. There are, supposedly, about nine hundred decorated megalithic stones in the world; six hundred of those are here in the Newgrange complex.

There are also some people who believe that Newgrange is not a burial site at all, but a ceremonial site used mostly for initiation rites. According to some ancient manuscripts, the builders of Newgrange and their descendants used to communicate with the spirits of the dead in religious rites. They would enter the tumulus and fast for three days and three nights, lying or squatting on the stone troughs in complete darkness. After the fast, communication would be achieved and the initiates would emerge into the light.

Symbolically, they entered the chamber, their minds in darkness and great knowledge was passed onto them during communication. They then emerged into the light with the newly acquired knowledge. There is a correlation here with one of the central themes of Christianity. The dead Christ stayed in his tomb for three days and then emerged alive. This idea is probably present in the practices of many of the ancient civilizations.

The River Boyne takes its name from the Goddess Boand. Her name means the "Goddess of the White Cow." It was a belief of the ancient people that each phase of the moon was represented by a different coloured animal. The story goes that the Boyne River sprang up when Boand, who had been forbidden to go near a certain secret well, approached the well. The waters rose up and engulfed her and flowed towards the sea. Boand became the river and the river is the goddess. Boand had borne the son of Dagda Mor, one of the greatest of all the De Danaan gods. The child's name was Aengus, the god of love. Aengus lived here in "The Palace" at Newgrange and is buried here.

The ancient *Book of Lecan* described the origins of Newgrange like this:

There was Eochaid Ollathair, The Dagda Mor,
son of Eladan, son of Delbaith, eighty years in the
Kingdom of Erin. It was he who had three sons,
    Aengus
and Aed and Cermaid. It was upon these four the
    men
of Erin made the Sidh of the Brugh.

Every time I enter the mound at Newgrange, I get goosebumps. The beauty, the artwork, the mystical pulse that throbs through the atmosphere, all combine to make Brugh Na Boinne—Newgrange, Knowth and Dowth, indeed the whole Boyne Valley—a magical place for me.

∗

MEMORIES

I remember very clearly, the first time I visited Newgrange. There had been a light drizzle of rain early in the day. As I drove north out of Dublin it began to ease off a bit and by the time I had reached Glasnevin Cemetery it had stopped. Approaching Finglas, the clouds had begun to move and patches of blue sky were appearing. On reaching open country the sun was shining gloriously, the harbinger of a beautiful day to come. In Slane I took the road to the right and following signs, made my way towards Newgrange. I had read about it but was not prepared for the magnificence of the building. Rounding the bends on the small country roads I caught a side view of it on my right and could not take my eyes off of it. On rounding the final bend and coming up on the full frontal view in the brilliant morning sunshine I was mesmerised! I barely remember paying the entrance fee and getting the little coloured sticker. On the walk across the field to the entrance I kept smiling to myself and gazing in wonder at the shining building.

As I walked, or rather floated, up the long passageway between the tall carved stones, with ten or twelve other people and our guide, the hairs on the back of my neck began to rise and tingle. With every step I took up into the chamber I was more and more convinced that I had been there before.

After our guide had given her talk about the various carvings, the stone basins and the corbelled roof, she asked if anyone had any questions. I said "There's a feather carved somewhere here." Where I got this information from I don't know, I certainly had not read it or heard it anywhere. Stepping away from where she had been standing and pointing it out on the megalith that had been at her back, she said "I nearly forgot about that. It's not a feather, it's a fern." I was dumbstruck!

Written on the Stones

Stones that stand in circles,
Circles carved on stone,
Sunlight shining through the earth,
Winds that sigh and moan
Singing hymns on mystic hills
By the river bend;
Seasons in their turning
From dark to light again.

> *Chorus:*
> See the stones! See the stones!
> The answers to the mysteries
> Are written on the stones.

Ancient masters carved them
Five thousand years gone by.
Knowledge scanned from Sol's bright course
And the starry sky.
Saving for posterity
Things that should be known;
Knowledge for the seeker
Carved upon a stone.

> *Chorus:*

—TOMMY MAKEM

William's Glen

If we take the road between the Brugh Na Boinne and the bend in Boand's river and travel northeast past Dowth, we come to William's Glen at Oldbridge. It's so called, because here on 1 July 1690 the soldiers of William of Orange, a prince of the Low Countries (Belgium and the Netherlands), defeated the soldiers of King James II of Scotland, for the throne of England. This famous battle has affected Irish history even to the present day.

A few miles up the road straight ahead, we would come to the town of Drogheda, where three thousand citizens were slain when Oliver Cromwell sacked the town in 1649. We are taking this little road to the left and it will lead us to Mellifont Abbey, near the village of Collon in County Louth.

The ruins of Mellifont Abbey, the first Cistercian monastery built in Ireland. (photo by Tommy Makem)

Mellifont Abbey

Mellifont Abbey, the first Cistercian monastery built in Ireland, was founded in 1142 by St. Malachy, who was archbishop of Armagh. The saint, born Malachy O'Morgair in the city of Armagh, travelled to France as a young monk. At the monastery in Clairvaux, where his good friend St. Bernard was abbot, he became very impressed by the monastery and its lifestyle. Later, Malachy sent a few of his novices to study life in Clairvaux and they, on returning to Ireland, formed the nucleus of the Mellifont community. Even the site on the Mattock River was chosen because of its similarity to Clairvaux.

The Abbey Church was consecrated in 1157 and under the orders of King Henry VIII was suppressed in 1539. It came into the possession of one Edward Moore, who was an ancestor to the earls of Drogheda. From him, it passed to the Balfour family of nearby Townley Hall. The Lavabo, which was built in the thirteenth century, was octagonal, but only four sides of it remain today. The Chapter House at Mellifont was built in the fourteenth century. It had two stories and a beautiful groined roof.

Tara

We take the Navan Road out of Slane and a few miles south of Navan, a little road to our right leads us to one of the most important places in Ireland—The Royal Hill of Tara.

Tara was the seat of the high kings of Ireland during its most glorious days, the first centuries A.D., but it was a place of importance since 2000 B.C. and remains a place of importance to the people of Ireland. After Christianity was introduced in Ireland, Tara's influence slowly declined, but it was not until 1022 that it was totally abandoned.

Tara, or Temair, as it's called in Irish, got its name from Tea, daughter of Lugaid, wife of Eremon. Eremon was the son of Mil of the Milesians, who invaded Ireland around 1200 B.C., and is reputedly buried here on Tara.

About the year 918 B.C., Ollamh Fodhla, aptly called the Solomon of Ireland, became the twenty-first Milesian king here at Tara. He reigned for forty years. Among the vast array of his achievements, he organized the nation for efficiency. Having divided the land into cantreds, districts containing a hundred townlands, he appointed a chief over every cantred, a magistrate over every territory, and a steward over every townland. He established a school of learning. His crowning glory is that he established the Feis at Tara, the great triennial Parliament of the chiefs, nobles and scholars of the nation, to settle the nation's affairs. This assembly was unique among the nations in those early ages and right down to Christian times.

It was from the laws made and discussed at these assemblies that the Brehon Laws took form. The Brehon Laws were conceived with a brilliancy in law-making that is unsurpassed to the present day. The scope of the Brehon Laws was astoundingly vast, covering every fine shade of relationship, social and moral, between two people. It covered everything from the laws defining all the different species of bargains, contracts and engagements between person and person through laws minutely regulating the fees of doctors, judges, lawyers and teachers, and all other professional people. Included were complete criminal laws respecting manslaughter and murder, distinguishing accurately between principals and accessories before and after the fact.

This gigantic body of ancient Irish legal literature still exists. Five large volumes have been printed, the principal part of these being the Senchus Mor, which was supposedly edited by St. Patrick, and named for him "The Statute Law of Patrick."

The Honourable John McCormick, the late, learned Speaker

of the House in the American House of Representatives, told me that the Magna Carta was based on the Brehon Laws. Since the Constitution of the United States is based on the Magna Carta, then the basic laws that govern the United States came from the brilliant minds of those ancient law-makers and poets at those assemblies at Tara.

Of all the kings who reigned at Tara, perhaps the most illustrious, after Ollamh Fodhla, was Cormac Mac Art who ascended the throne in A.D. 224. It was he who built all the wooden structures, the palaces and halls mentioned in early literature, the outlines of which still remain. These include Cormac's House, the Royal Enclosure and the Great Banquet Hall. The ancient poets wrote of Tara:

> Temair, noblest of hills,
> Under which is Erin of the forays,
> The lofty city of Cormac, son of Art,
> Son of mighty Conn of the Hundred Fights.
>
> Cormac, constant was his prosperity,
> He was sage, he was poet, he was prince;
> He was a true judge of the men of Fene.
> He was a friend, he was a comrade.
>
> Cormac, who gained fifty fights,
> Disseminated the Psalter of Temair;
> In this Psalter there is
> All the best we have of history.

—FROM *1000 YEARS OF IRISH POETRY*

The great Banquet Hall that Cormac Mac Art built is a most interesting structure. It was also known as "The House of Mead Circling," and was about 750 feet long and 75 feet wide. Ancient manuscripts describe it as being a rectangular wooden building divided into aisles and compartments. Each grade of society or class of person had their correct place designated in the hall and the proper colours in their clothing. The approved cut of meat suitable to their station in life was also laid out by the Laws of Hospitality.

In the matter of clothing the following colours were allowed: The king or queen could wear seven colours; the poet 6; the chieftain 5; army leader 4; land owner 3; rent payer 2; and serf, one colour only.

In sacredness of person, the king usually held next place to the poet. The lives of kings were frequently taken, but seldom, if ever, did the sacrilegious killing of a poet occur.

According to a poem translated from the Irish by Edward Gwynn, the cuts of meat at the banquet were allotted as follows:

> The House of Temair, round which is the rath,
> From it was given each his due;
> Honour still continues to such as them
> At the courts of kings and princes.

> King and Chief of the Poets,
> Sage farmer, they received their due,
> Couches that torches burn not,
> The thighs and the chine-steaks.

> Leech and spencer, stout smith,
> Steward, portly butler,
> The heads of the beasts to all of them
> In the house of the yellow-haired king.

> Engraver, famed architect,
> Shield maker and keen soldier,
> In the King's house, they drank a cup;
> This was the special right of their hands.

Jester, chess-player, sprawling buffoon,
Piper, cheating juggler,
The shank was their share of meat in truth,
When they came to the King's house.

The shins were the share of the noble musician,
Of the castle-builder and artificer, round the bowl,
The cup-bearer, the lusty foot servant,
Both consumed the broken meats.

A charge on the Prince of Meath,
Were the cobblers and combmakers,
The due of the strong skilled folk
Was the fat underside of the shoulder.

The backs, the chines in every dwelling
Were given to Druids and Doorkeepers.
There was protection for maidens with never an
    "ach!"
After serving the House of Tara.

Edward Gwynn also translated this from the Irish of some ancient poet:

Perished is every law concerning high fortune,
Crumbled to the clay is every ordinance;
Tara, though she be desolate today,
Once on a time was the habitation of heroes.

Tara reigned supreme in glory down the centuries. In the hearts and minds of the people of Ireland it remains glorious and mystical.

MEMORIES

Driving north on the main Dublin to Derry road, I saw the one and only signpost, or as we used to call them, fingerpost, pointing the way to Tara. This being one of the most important places in Ireland, I was telling myself off for not having visited it before now and decided—no time like the present. Turning left, I was proceeding along the little country road looking for more signposts indicating the way to Tara. After many turnings and many miles without seeing another sign, I was becoming more and more annoyed with the powers that be who did not think enough of this national treasure to put up a few signs for visitors. Eventually I met a friendly postman delivering his mail who gave me directions to the Navan Road where I found another signpost. It was most assuredly worth the trouble when I finally reached the hallowed hill. Don't be put off if you're having difficulty finding the way to Royal Tara; just ask any of the friendly people you'll meet along the roads.

2

CUCHULLAIN COUNTRY

Ardee

The main Dublin to Derry road runs through Slane, Collon and then into Ardee in County Louth. The name Ardee comes from the Irish "Ath Fhirdia," which means Ferdia's Ford. During the mythological epic *An Tain Bo Culaigne* (The Cattle Raid of Cooley), the magnificent Ulster hero Cuchullain fought his great friend Ferdia in single combat here for three days. Each night after their fighting, the two heroes shared food, talked of their early days together and had their wounds healed with herbs and potions, which were applied by their charioteers.

On the third day of their battle, Cuchullain killed his dearest friend with his magic spear The Gae Bolga. Cuchullain, though severely wounded, carried his friend's body across to the northern bank of the River Dee. He wanted to pay him homage for having died the glorious death of a warrior hero. In the eyes of his friends, Ferdia was seen to have crossed the river which Cuchullain was defending.

In the town of Ardee there are two thirteenth-century castles. One was built by Roger de Pippard to mark the Anglo-Norman occupation of the town. It has been restored and houses a small museum and also serves as a courthouse. The other is called Hatch's Castle.

MEMORIES

Dermot O'Brien, a fine fellow musician, told me a lovely little incident that illustrates how the good people of Ireland will not allow anyone to get too full of their own importance.

Back in the mid 1960s Dermot had recorded a song that was getting lots of airplay on Radio Eireann, the national radio station. It became a hit recording for him.

On a visit to his hometown of Ardee, Dermot was walking down the street when he was greeted by an older denizen of the town:

"Come 'eer, what's your name?"

"O'Brien."

"Are you the musician fellow?"

"I suppose you could call me that."

"Heard you on the wireless a Tuesday."

"That's nice to hear."

"Heard you on a Wednesday as well."

"I hope you enjoyed it."

"You were far better a Tuesday!"

Cuchullain's Stone where Cuchullain stood mortally wounded, but determined to die on his feet as he faced his enemies. (photo by Tommy Makem)

Knockbridge

About ten miles northeast of Ardee we come to Knockbridge. Just east of the road to Dundalk at Ratheddy, stands the twelve-foot-high Cuchullain Stone. It was here that the fatally wounded Cuchullain, surrounded by many enemies, tied himself to a stone pillar, so he should die on his feet. His enemies were so afraid of him that they would not dare approach the body until The Morrigan, the Goddess of War, in the form of a raven, came and perched on his shoulder. Then, and only then, they knew he was dead and dared, though very timidly, to draw near.

Dundalk

Dundalk is a charming, flourishing business town with a busy seaport. The area has been renowned since mythological times. Castletown Hill to the west of the town is reputed to be the birthplace of Cuchullain. The spot was called Dun Dealgan (Delga's Fort) and that is where Dundalk got its name.

In the thirteenth century it was a garrison town and remains so today. In A.D. 1220 King John, the brother of Richard the Lion-Hearted, made the town a borough. There was a Franciscan friary established here in 1240. The Arctic explorer Sir Francis Mc Clintock was born in Seatown Place.

It is a very busy town about halfway between Dublin and Belfast. Among many cultural events it can boast an International Amateur Drama Festival held annually in May. The Dundalk Horse Races and the Greyhound Race Track help to bring many visitors to this bustling, exciting town.

Proleek Dolmen with its forty-ton capstone. (photo by Tommy Makem)

Carlingford

At Ballymacscanlon, we find the very fine Proleek Dolmen with a forty-ton capstone, which dates from 2000 B.C. Local tradition has it that if you throw three pebbles on to the capstone and they stay, your wish will come true.

Stay on the little road beside the dolmen and we can climb up into the legendary Cooley Mountains. They are renowned as the setting for *An Tain Bo Culaigne* (The Cattle Raid of Cooley), the greatest epic in Irish mythology.

From the top of the Cooley Mountains we have a beautiful view of Dundalk Bay. Down the other side of the mountain Carlingford Lough is at our feet. The Mountains of Mourne rise majestically on the far side of the bay, or lough as it's called. To our right, the port of Greenore is always busy with container ships plying their trade around the world. A couple of miles north of Greenore is the ancient town of Carlingford. I wrote a song about it one time.

Farewell to Carlingford

When I was young and in my prime,
And could wander wild and free,
There was always a longing in my mind
To follow the call of the sea.

   Chorus:
   So I'll sing farewell to Carlingford,
   And farewell to Greenore,
   I'll think of you both day and night
   Until I return once more,
   Until I return once more.

On all of the stormy seven seas
I have sailed before the mast,
And on every voyage I ever made
I swore it would be my last.

   Chorus:

I had a girl called Mary Doyle
And she lived in Greenore,
And the foremost thought that was in her mind
Was to keep me safe on shore.

   Chorus:

Now the landsman's life is all his own.
He can go or he can stay,
But when the sea gets in your blood
When she calls you must obey.

   Chorus:

—TOMMY MAKEM

A view of King John's Castle in Carlingford on an ominously cloudy day. (photo by Tommy Makem)

Viking raiders gave the lough and the village their names. They recognized the strategic strength of the place, so they built a fortified trading centre from where they could move freely, by land or by sea, to harass and plunder the surrounding countryside. The castle ruin that dominates the town is King John's Castle, built in the early thirteenth century.

There is a small building in the village that is supported by an arch. The building is called the Tholsel and it is where the village leaders used to meet. In the eighteenth century, it also served as a jail. The arch that supports the building was part of the town wall, and originally, one of the town gates. Just a few yards down the narrow Tholsel Street, going towards the village square is the Mint, a tower house of the fifteenth to sixteenth century, with an extended turret over the door. The mullioned windows are remarkable for their carved Celtic motifs. A little farther on past the square is a sixteenth-century fortified town house called Taffe's Castle. On the other side of the Thosel are the remains of a fourteenth-century Dominican friary.

Carlingford's most famous son is Thomas Darcy McGee, born here in 1825. He went to America to visit an aunt in Providence, Rhode Island, when he was seventeen and made a speech there on 4 July that landed him an offer of a job on a Boston newspaper called *The Pilot*. He became its editor at the age of nineteen. McGee was such a wonderful orator that news of his oratory spread to Ireland and he was offered a job in Dublin on *The Freeman's Journal,* where he worked for a short time, before moving to *The Nation*. Because of his activities with the Young Ireland Movement, a price was put on his head, but disguised as a priest, he escaped and returned to America. On his return to America, he founded a publication also called *The Nation,* and later in Boston, he started *The American Celt.*

In 1858, he went to Canada, where he was elected to the Canadian Parliament from Montreal. Very quickly, he climbed the ladder of success, becoming in 1862, president of the Executive Council and later, minister of Agriculture. He was assassinated in Ottawa on 7 April 1868. There is a little plaza built in his honour in Carlingford. Having been born here, in Cuchullain country, it is no wonder that McGee would write:

Celts

Long, long ago, beyond the misty space
    Of twice a thousand years,
In Erin old there dwelt a mighty race
    Taller than Roman spears;
Like oaks and towers they had a giant grace,
    Were fleet as deers,
With wind and waves they made their 'biding
    place,
    These western shepherd seers.
Great was their deeds, their passions and their
    spirits;

> With clay and stone
> They piled on strath and shore those mystic forts,
>   Not yet o'erthrown;
> On cairn crowned hills they held their council-
>   courts;
>   While youths alone,
> With giant dogs, explored the elk resorts,
>   And brought them down.

With lovely old pubs and good restaurants, the village is alive with conversation and music. They have a yearly oyster festival and a yearly folk festival, two highlights in a crowded social calendar. Carlingford has been designated the first heritage town in Ireland.

Slieve Gullion

If we flew north and slightly west, with the wise and eternal crows, we'd come to Slieve Gullion in South Armagh, the most mystical of Irish mountains according to writer Standish O'Grady. The poets W. B. Yeats and AE were both enchanted by it. There are many tales of how it got its name.

The most prevalent theory is that it is named for Cullan the Smith, whose fierce guard dog was killed by the boy, Setanta, when he arrived at Cullan's fort after the gates had been closed. There was a feast in progress, which Cullan had given to honour Conor MacNessa, the king of Ulster, who ruled at Emhain Macha, the royal seat at Armagh. The large guard dog was making his rounds when he saw the young boy approach and ran to attack him. Setanta, who had run all the way from Emhain Macha with his hurley and hurling ball, was so skilled that he drove the hurling ball down the throat of the attacking dog and killed him. The roistering warriors at the feast heard the agonized howl of the dying dog and rushed outside to find out the cause of the commotion. They found the young boy standing over the remains of the fierce dog. Setanta was deeply sorry for having destroyed the protector of Cullan's fort and said he would undertake the duties of the hound until Cullan could find and train a new dog. Cathbad the Druid proclaimed that henceforth, the boy's name would be Cuchullain, the hound of Cullan.

Ossian the poet and Finn the heroic leader of the Fianna were closely associated with Slieve Gullion and, reputedly, somewhere on its slopes is where Deirdre of the Sorrows was reared in deep seclusion by Lavarcham the nurse.

The notorious Calliagh Bearra or Cally Barry as she's known locally, is the figure most associated with Slieve Gullion. Her "house," as it's called, is on top of the mountain beside Cally Barry's Lake, which according to local folklore, is bottomless. Her "house" is really a cruciform passage grave and cupola cairn, which has some features likened to stone monuments found in Spain and Portugal. As a youngster, I had often heard that when there were clouds on top of Slieve Gullion, they were really puffs of steam rising as Cally Barry was boiling her pot.

The circle of foothills around Slieve Gullion is known as The Ring of Gullion and was formed by volcanic eruption in the Tertiary period some 40 to 70 million years ago. Lava boiled up through the cracks to harden into jagged hills forming the ring. As the Ice Age receded, it left a tail of crags stretching as far as the village of Dromintee. This is one of the longest glacier tails in these islands.

All around Slieve Gullion's foot, poetry and music flourished. There was a noted school of poets in these parts that produced poets in the Irish language like Art McCooey and Peadar O'Dornain. Poetry, music and storytelling are alive and thriving still around the foot of this most mystical of Irish mountains.

Slieve Fuaid

Travelling north in a straight line from Slieve Gullion, we pass through the heart of the Fews Forest. This is the road that the boy Setanta would have taken on his way from his home in Dun Dealgan to Emhain Macha in Armagh to join the famed boy troop. In the Fews Forest, we come to the prominence nowadays called Carrickatuke. In Irish mythology, this is the eminent Slieve Fuad. St. Patrick had started to build his first church here, because of its reputation as a place of great importance to the Druids who gathered there; however, on looking down the valley to where the city of Armagh now stands, he was made aware of the power and influence that still emanated from where the storied Emhain Macha had stood. To partake of that great power for his church, he moved his building to where St. Patrick's Anglican Cathedral now stands on land given to him by the chieftain Daire.

According to Standish O'Grady, King Lir, of the Tuatha De Danaan, supposedly had his palace on Slieve Fuaid, the Hill of the White Field. He had four children, a girl Fionnuala, and three boys, Aedh, Fiachra and Conn, all of whom he loved very dearly. When his wife, Niamh, the mother of the children died, he married her sister Aoife, who possessed great magical powers. Shortly after she had married Lir, Aoife grew more and more dangerously jealous of the king's deep love for his children.

Unable to kill them, because they were of the De Danaan race, in a fit of anger and jealousy, she put a spell on them. The spell changed the children into four swans and condemned them to spend three hundred years on Lake Derravaragh, in County Westmeath; three hundred years on the Sea of Moyle, the straits between the northeast coast of Antrim and Scotland; and three hundred years in the waters around Inish Glora, off the west coast of Ireland. The swans retained human speech and sang hauntingly beautiful songs of their people, the Tuatha De Danaan. Their singing was so wondrous and enchanting, that their songs could make people who heard them cry, or dance with joy. They could melt ice or calm the seas and the storms. All of the creatures of sea and land and sky would gather to hear them and listen in wonder.

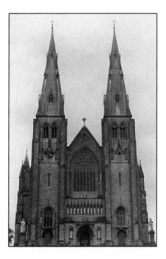

St. Patrick's Cathedral in Armagh marks the ecclesiastical capital of Ireland. (photo by Tommy Makem)

Armagh

When St. Patrick first saw Armagh, he cried out "It is Armagh that I love, my sweet thorp [village or small town], my sweet hill." He established his see here in A.D. 444 and so for the past 1,500 years, Armagh has been the ecclesiastical capital of Ireland. It is the primatial see of both the Catholic and Anglican Churches.

Armagh is undoubtedly one of the most venerated cities in Ireland and has been a centre of culture and learning since time immemorial. Rome, Barcelona and Armagh were known as the three great cultural centres of Europe. Arsene Darmesteter, the medievalist scholar, said "Armagh, the ecclesiastical capital of Ireland, was at one time the metropolis of civilization." Armagh sent scholars and missionaries to the known world and students came from all over Europe to study here. Indeed, at one point, there were so many students from England studying in Armagh, that part of the city was named the Saxon ward.

In A.D. 1004, Brian Boru, the high king of Ireland, came to Armagh. While visiting St. Patrick's Cathedral, he was done the honour of being allowed to hold the precious *Book of Armagh*. While kneeling at the altar, holding the book, the wonder of it impressed him so much, that he donated twenty ounces of pure gold in tribute. Ten years later, just after King Brian's victory over the Danes at Clontarf in Dublin, in A.D. 1014, the king and his son were killed in their tent and both bodies were brought to Armagh and buried at the cathedral.

The *Book of Armagh* is a Latin manuscript of the New Testament, combined with the confessions of St. Patrick, two accounts of the life of St. Patrick and various other writings translated by the scribe Ferdomnach in A.D. 807. In an ancient leather satchel, inscribed with Celtic designs, the *Book of Armagh* is kept in the Library in Trinity College, Dublin.

Another great treasure from Armagh, is the Shrine of St. Patrick's Bell. The bell is made of iron plates bronzed on both sides, which are riveted together, and engraved with a request for a prayer for Cumascach, who was a steward of the Monastery of Armagh, and who died in A.D. 908. The shrine, which contains the bell, was commissioned some time between A.D. 1094 and 1105. It is made of bronze and silver plates, ornamented with enamel, gold filigree work and crystal. Both the bell and the shrine are in the National Museum in Dublin, along with the Loughnashade Trumpet, a Bronze Age instrument found at Loughnashade in the Emhain Macha complex, two miles west of Armagh.

St. Malachy (Malachy O'Morgair) was born in Armagh and later became its archbishop. He founded the first Cistercian monastery in Ireland at Mellifont, County Louth, in A.D. 1142.

In the year A.D. 684, Prince Aldfrid, who was educated in Ireland and was later to become king of the Northumbrian Saxons, wrote in his *Itinerary Through Ireland:*

> I found in Armagh the splendid,
> Meekness, wisdom, circumspection,
> Fasting in obedience to the Son of God,
> Noble, prosperous sages.

This is a literal translation, by John O'Donovan, in the mid-nineteenth century, from the original.

Not only is Armagh a city with roots very deeply planted in the cultural identity of Ireland, but with its world renowned observatory, built in A.D. 1789, and its planetarium, it has its head high among the stars of the earth's future. It is a lovely, tranquil city. As we walk the streets of a very modern Armagh, we know through the atmosphere that permeates our bones, that we are walking very ancient paths.

MEMORIES

The city of Armagh, to me, will always be associated with a dark green, very comfortable diesel bus. Its seats were covered in leather and it had an efficient circular heater attached to the front of the interior of the bus, on the panel that separated the driver's compartment from the passengers. It smelled of leather with a light dash of diesel fumes; just like a bus should smell. It was usually full as it took very happy dancers from Keady to big ceilidhs (pronounced kay-lees) in the City Hall in Armagh. Ceilidh dancing meant strictly Irish dances like the Sixteen Hand Reel or the Haymakers Jig. Not even old-time waltzes were allowed. The music was usually supplied by the McCusker Brothers Ceilidh Band. The McCuskers were nine local brothers, well known nationally, who made the sweetest music in the land. Armagh's ancient winding streets and the music of the McCusker Brothers were made for each other. With all of her lovely Georgian architecture and her airs of sophistication, Armagh still has an ancient cultural aura about her that neither time nor human effort can erase.

Armagh also conjures up very enjoyable days playing hurling and football; happy evenings strolling her streets or going to the "pictures" at the Ritz or the Cosy Corner; friendship and "crack" over an exotic cup of coffee at the Rainbow Cafe, owned and operated by the amiable Tommy McAvinchey; fish and chips in a paper bag with lots of brown vinegar from Caffola's; riding home on the Keady bus with Paddy Greene driving and the affable Bob McKindry conducting, or maybe Joey Beattie and Frankie Treanor.

Armagh is another world. The memories of her are a very big part of my youth.

The celebrated hill of Emhain Macha, setting of the great Ulster Cycle of Tales. (photo by Tommy Makem)

Emhain Macha

The name Armagh comes from the Irish Ard Macha, which means Macha's Height or Hill. It was named for the warrior Queen Macha, who reputedly built the renowned Palace of Emhain Macha (pronounced avan macha) a couple miles west of the present city of Armagh. There are two different stories of how Emhain Macha was named, and there are two different Machas involved in the stories.

The first was Macha Mong Ruad (Macha the Red-Haired), who was the first Milesian queen of Ireland. Her father was Aodh Ruad, one of three kings, who by mutual consent, took seven-year turns in reigning. The other two were Dithorba and Cimbaoth. Aodh Ruad was drowned at Eas Aodh Ruad (Assaroe), which is the present day Ballyshannon, in County Donegal. When his turn came around again to rule, his daughter Macha claimed the throne. She had to fight her father's two partners for the privilege. During the battle, she killed Dithorba and afterwards, defeated and then married Cimbaoth and made him king. Cimbaoth's reign roughly coincided with that of Alexander the Great, about 330 B.C.

When Cimbaoth died, Queen Macha took up the reigns of government herself. She took the gold brooch from her tunic, walked down from the top of the hill, and with the pin of her brooch, traced out on the earth the circles and lines on which she wanted her residence built. She then set the captives she had captured in battle to build her magnificent palace. For almost seven hundred years, the great stronghold of Emhain Macha was to be the Royal House of the Kings of Ulster, and was to play a most important part in the fortunes of not only Ulster, but of Ireland.

The second story of how Emhain Macha got its name appeals to me personally, even more than the first. The son of Agnoman, Crunnchu, whose wife had died, lived in a remote area of the mountains. One day, a strange and very beautiful woman came to his house, started to work and stayed. She was an invaluable help to Crunnchu and made him a wonderful wife. He prospered. Crunnchu's new wife was none other than the Goddess Macha. Macha was, supposedly, one manifestation of the Triple Goddess. The other two aspects of the triune were Morrigan and Badbh. Collectively, they represented youth, maturity and old age.

At a gathering of the Ulster Warriors, the bards sang the praises of the king's horses. Chrunnchu, who had been enjoying many large cups of ale at the feast, said his wife, who had almost come to the fullness of her time in pregnancy, could outrun the king's horses. The king, on hearing this remark, bid Crunnchu's wife to be brought before him and to fulfill the challenge her husband had laid down. The woman protested vigorously, saying "Have compassion. How many of you would permit your wives or mothers to suffer this indignity?" The warriors, aroused by their carousing and fortified with large quantities of ale, all roared for the completion of the challenge. The king joined with the warriors, saying "If you do not race against my horses, Crunnchu will forfeit his life."

Macha won the race, but at the finish line, delivered twins, a boy and a girl, screaming in horrendous agony. The place was called Emhain Macha for Macha's twins. In her terrible pain and suffering, Macha put a curse on the warriors of Ulster, that in the time of their greatest trial and need, they would suffer the pains and pangs of childbirth to the ninth generation. The story is the first in the epic tale *An Tain Bo Culaigne* (The Cattle Raid of Cooley). The curse that Macha put on the Ulster warriors was to have tremendous repercussions on the outcome of that phenomenal epic.

Emhain Macha is where the great Ulster Cycle of Tales was set. These tales are, undoubtedly, Ireland's most important contribution to medieval literature. Here's where the exploits of Cuchullain and the glorious Red Branch Knights were centered. Cuchullain's magic sword, which was called Caladbolg, is reputedly the original of King Arthur's sword Excalibur. The Red Branch Knights got their name from the branches of the redwood trees, with which the Great Hall at Emhain Macha was built. These, I am told, are the same sort of redwoods that are still found in Muir Woods in San Francisco. Here at Emhain Macha, the magnificent legend of Deirdre of the Sorrows and the Sons of Uisneach was set. This is where King Conor Mac-Nessa's fierce jealousy smouldered, grew and bred the treachery that would leave Emhain Macha in flames and turned to dust.

The palace at Emhain Macha consisted of three houses: the Royal House, the Speckled House and the House of the Red Branch.

The Royal House had 150 rooms, built with red yew wood which was fastened with copper rivets. The king's room had the red yew walls faced with copper and silver and decorated with gold birds, their heads inset with precious stones. There were nine partitions in the king's chambers stretching from the fire to the wall. Each partition was thirty feet high. King Conor MacNessa had a silver rod to which were attached three golden apples. When the king struck the rod and made it resound, the household had to be silent. His magic shield was called The Ochain, which means The Moaning One. If the king was ever in danger the shield would moan and the shields of all the warriors in Ulster would answer.

The Speckled House was where the heroes of the Red Branch kept their swords, shields and spears. Because of the brightness and colours of the hilts of the swords, the spears with bands of silver and gold, the gold and silver on the bosses and rims of the shields, and because of the drinking cups and horns, the place was almost moving with sparkle and glitter. This is why it was so appropriately named The Speckled House.

The House of the Red Branch was where the warriors kept the severed heads and spears of their beaten enemies.

At the end of the tragic story of Deirdre of the Sorrows when the Sons of Uisneach returned from Scotland to Emhain

Macha they were treacherously killed. In the ensuing fighting Emhain Macha was burned to the ground. Its glory and splendour were wafted away in the smoke. That was in A.D. 331, when Muredach II ruled as high king on Tara.

Emhain Macha is still a very important place. According to Professor J. P. Mallory of Queen's University in Belfast, this legendary hill is not only one of the most important archaeological sites in Europe, it is the only site in Ireland to show in detail a continuity of occupation across the period from 700 to 100 B.C. This is the period in which most scholars believe the first Irish-speaking Celts colonized Ireland.

This small green hill still shimmers with the glory, the splendour and the spirits of the magnificent heroes and heroines who peopled it in the misty ages past. The aura lingers.

3

THE ANCIENT KINGDOM OF MOURNE

Newry

Leaving the city of Armagh we climb a steep hill with Dobbin's Flowery Vale on our left, and the old wall of the Archbishop's Palace Demesne on our right.

Dobbin's Flowery Vale

One evening fair when Phoebus bright her radiant
smiles displayed,
When Flora in her verdant garb the flagrant plains
arrayed,
As I did rove throughout each grove, no care did
me assail,
A pair I spied by a riverside in Dobbin's Flowery
Vale.

There I sat down for to behold beneath a spread-
ing tree,
The limpid streams that gently rolled conveyed
their words to me:
"Farewell sweet maid" the youth he said "since I
must now set sail

And bid adieu to Armagh, you and Dobbin's Flowery Vale.

"Forbear those thoughts and cruel words that
  wound a bleeding heart,
For is it true that we're met here alas! so soon to
  part?
Must I alone here sigh and moan, to none my grief
  reveal,
But here lament my cause to vent in Dobbin's
  Flowery Vale?

"Do not reflect that you're alone, nor yet am I untrue,
If ever I should chance to roam my thoughts will
  be on you;
There's not a flower in shady bower, on verdant
  hill or dale,
But will me remind, of the maid behind in Dobbin's Flowery Vale."

It's mutual love together drew them with a kind
  embrace,
While tears like rosy drops of dew did trickle down
  her face;
She tried in vain him to detain, and while she did
  bewail,
He bade adieu, and I withdrew from Dobbin's
  Flowery Vale.

—ANONYMOUS

We're on the Newry Road, a modern highway undulating between rolling hills and well-tended fields. Passing the town of
Markethill, very soon Slieve Gullion looms up on our right and
the majestic Mountains of Mourne beckon straight ahead in

the blue hazy distance. Down in the hollow is the bustling town of Newry.

Newry has always been a thriving business centre with access to the sea. Merchant ships brought coal and lumber and many other commodities right into the town via the canal. The Newry Canal was the first major inland waterway built in either Ireland or Britain. It has been a water artery since 1741, and there is some talk of it being refurbished and reopened for pleasure boating in the future.

While commercial life thrived in Newry, the arts were certainly not forgotten. In 1742, Handel gave a performance of "Alexander's Feast" here. The famous Smock Alley Theatre from Dublin performed here frequently and by 1769 Newry had its own theatre in High Street. At the present time, the flourishing drama and musical societies of the town have individual festivals of their own. A new arts centre has been opened.

For his leadership role in the Young Ireland Movement in the mid-1800s, John Mitchel, a Newry man, was deported to Van Dieman's Land, a penal colony off the south east coast of Australia. It is now called Tasmania. Mitchel wrote and published a famous chronicle called *John Mitchel's Jail Journal*. On his return from Van Dieman's Land he was elected to Parliament. He died in Newry in 1875. His statue stands in John Mitchel Place.

The poet John Kells Ingram was born in Hill Street. He was made a Fellow of Trinity College in Dublin in 1846. Later he was appointed professor of Greek, professor of English literature and senior lecturer, ultimately serving as vice-provost. Ingram was president of the Royal Irish Academy and wrote articles on slavery and political economy for the *Encyclopædia Brittanica.*

Lord Russell of Killowen, chief justice of England from 1894 to 1900, was born in Newry in 1832. There is a very striking bust of him in the vestibule of the Town Hall, a gift of the English Law Society.

Newry, with a long tradition of commerce, and noted for its markets, like the Butter Market, the Corn Market and the Pig Market, still has the best Variety Market you'll find anywhere. It has all the colour, excitement, dynamism, humour and character that epitomizes this town. Singer, songwriter Colm Sands summed up the market in this line from his song about it: "Newry Market has it all from an anchor to a pin."

Rostrevor

The six-lane highway that runs along the Clanrye River and past Narrow-Water Castle, takes us to the popular seaside resort of Warrenpoint. In recent years, Warrenpoint has become a very busy container port. In 1823, the noted poet Thomas Caulfield Irwin, who was known throughout Europe as the Wordsworth of Ireland, was born in Warrenpoint.

Travelling along the waterfront for a couple of miles, we melt into the peaceful atmosphere of Rostrevor. This lovely town is named for the Ross family, one of whom, it is said, was in charge of the English troops who burned what was to become known as the White House in Washington, D.C., on 4 August 1814. There is an obelisk in memory of the Ross family as you enter the town from Warrenpoint.

On the road from Rostrevor to the fishing centre of Kilkeel is Ballyedmond Castle. The trees in its beautiful grounds are planted in the same formations as the regiments at the battle of Waterloo, the final and decisive battle in the Napoleonic Wars. The battle was fought at Waterloo, Belgium, on 18 June 1815.

Perhaps the best known landmark in the Rostrevor area is The Cloughmore, a great boulder up on Slieve Ban. As the story goes, two giants were fighting each other across Carlingford Lough. Finn Toirneach on Slieve Foy, the southern shore of the lough and Ruiscaire, the Giant of Ice and Winter here on the northern shore. They fought for three days. On the first day they fought with swords, neither gaining the upper hand. On the second day they fought with clubs and, again, neither one could prevail. The third day they fought with rocks. Both of them were exhausted and at length Finn, summoning the last remnants of his great strength for one last tremendous effort, lifted the Cloghmore, hurled it across the lough and crushed Ruiscaire. If we were to examine the loose rocks on Slieve Ban, we would find that they are the type of rock belonging to Slieve Foy and vice versa. Ever since that great fight, the space over the lough between the two mountains has been called Ceim Cloice (The Stone Throw). Finn Toirneach was a warm friendly giant and his defeat of Ruiscaire represents the passing of the Ice Age from Ireland. Finn Toirneach, by the way, still sleeps on Slieve Foy. We can see his outline across the way, with his head on top of the mountain and his feet in the water below.

I have always considered Rostrevor to be a very lovely place and have written a song about it.

The Town of Rostrevor

The sun in the morning came over the mountain
And the thrush and the linnet they were singing in
    each tree,
And as I walked along, well I thought I'd find glory
If I'd list in the army, a soldier lad to be.

Chorus:
Oh, I'm going back to the town of Rostrevor
Where the gentle rippling waters meet the
mighty Mourne shore,
And whenever I return I will stay there for ever
In the town of Rostrevor with the girl I do adore.

They gave me a hat and a fine coat of scarlet
And the sergeant came up and put a musket in my
    hand.

He taught me to drill and to march in formation,
And obey all my orders, whatever he'd command.

Chorus:

The fifes sweetly played and the drums they did
     rattle,
On a ship then we sailed far across the raging sea.
The cannons they did roar and the wars they were
     cruel,
Oh hard is the life of a soldier lad like me.

Chorus:

My time it is up and I'm leaving tomorrow,
After three years of hardships once more I will be
     free,
So farewell to the guns, and the drilling and the
     marching
And when I get back home, no more soldiering for
     me.

Chorus:

—Tommy Makem

The Kingdom of Mourne

All around the coast on the Mourne shore shepherds, fishermen, farmers and stonecutters abound. They are kind, warm,
welcoming folk with great songs and stories, especially of the
sea and its legends. Mourne granite and stonecutters are
renowned around the world.

   In Kilkeel, the capital of the Kingdom of Mourne, they say

that the tides which circle Ireland all meet. Their ebbing and flowing leaves an abundance of plankton that attracts fish in large numbers. It is no wonder that they boast of having the largest fishing fleet in Ireland. The wonderful sight of the fleet at anchor, particularly on weekends, attracts thousands of visitors.

Oh! the mountains themselves; always mystical, exciting, majestic and beautiful. Wonderful names, too: Fionlieve, the fair mountain; Shan Slieve, the old mountain; The Clocking Hen; Slieve Binnian, the peaked mountain; Ben Crom, named after the old Celtic God of Darkness.

Cradled up in the Mournes, the beautiful Silent Valley was dammed up to become a water supply for the people of Mourne and with the Ben Crom Dam, a water supply for the city of Belfast. Slieve Donard, the highest peak in the Mournes at 2,795 feet, dips its feet in Dundrum Bay and holds the town of Newcastle in its lap. Named for Donard of Maghera, a monk who built his oratory on the peak, it had previously been called Slanga after the son of Parthalon, who had been drowned in Dundrum Bay.

Parthalon was the leader of the group of people who colonized Ireland around 2035 B.C. They came from Scythia in southwest Europe and adjoining parts of Asia. Named for their leader, the Parthalonians were in Ireland for between three and four hundred years. They were eventually destroyed by a plague.

Newcastle is ideally situated on Dundrum Bay with nearly five miles of sandy beach. Slieve Donard stands sentry over it. It has been a popular seaside and spa resort since time out of memory. For the golfing enthusiast, the Royal County Down course is a paradise to even the most demanding.

Downpatrick

Downpatrick is situated to the northeast of Dundrum Bay. In the graveyard of the Church of Ireland Cathedral, Ireland's three pre-eminent saints, Patrick, Brigid and Colmcille (Columba) are buried.

In A.D. 432, on his return to Ireland, St. Patrick is said to have landed at the mouth of the River Slaney or as it is now called Fiddler's Burn. One of his first converts was the local chieftain Dichu, who gave him land to erect a church at Saul.

The remains of Inch Abbey stand on the banks of the River Quoile. It was built by John de Courcy in atonement for the total destruction of Erenagh Abbey by the raiding Vikings. Erenagh Abbey was a much earlier monastic settlement on the same site.

Downpatrick is a lovely town of late Georgian and early Victorian buildings and charming roads like the cobbled English Street which climbs the hill to the cathedral. The town is historically connected to the insurrection of 1798.

Thomas Russell, a very close friend of the very influential Mc Cracken family of Belfast, was hanged in Downpatrick for his part in organizing the United Irishmen who fought in that rebellion. Russell's memory has been immortalized in Florence Wilson's wonderful monologue "The Man From God Knows Where" which ends:

> He bowed his head to the swinging rope,
> And I said "Please God" to his dying hope
> And "Amen" to his dying prayer,
> That the wrongs might cease and the rights prevail,
> For that man they hanged at Downpatrick Jail
> Was the Man From God Knows Where.

Bangor

Bangor is a modern, thriving, go-ahead seaside resort on the northwest coast of County Down. It has been welcoming and entertaining countless visitors down through the years. Enticing and modern though it is, I always think of Bangor as an ancient place. Because of a monastery founded here by St. Comgall in A.D. 555, it has been called "The Light of the World." It was known as Bangor Mor (Big Bangor) to distinguish it from Bangor in Wales. St. Comgall's monastery was a dominant seat of ecclesiastic high learning. Some of the greatest names in Irish religious history were educated in Bangor including Saints Columbanus, Gall, Moluag, Maebrubha and Malachy. Scholarly holy men were sent out from Bangor to spread Christianity all over the known world. They established monasteries throughout the very heart of Europe. Towns and cities sprang up and flourished around these monasteries. The monks left the shores of Bangor with nothing between them and the stormy seas but the thin hides of their coracles and their unshakeable faith.

The monastic settlement at Bangor consisted of a number of wattle huts surrounding the church, refectory, school and hospice. Life was severe. Food was scarce and milk was considered an indulgence. They had one meal a day and that was not served until evening. Silence was demanded at mealtimes and at other times talk was kept to a minimum. Work was hard and learning very intense.

St. Cumgall's monastery had pupils from all over Europe. It became so renowned and rich, that it was attacked and raided by brigands and robbers often, and with varying amounts of savagery. Later, the Norsemen came by sea and found rich plunder here. The most savage attack by the Vikings was a massive assault in the year A.D. 824 when upwards of three thousand people were killed, and the monastery completely wrecked. Manuscripts and anything that was not considered useful by the marauders were destroyed and the entire settlement left in ruins. St. Malachy of Armagh came to Bangor in A.D. 1121 and was so horrified by what he found that he vowed he would restore the monastery to its former glory. Unfortunately, he died before he had completed his task.

Choral antiphonal singing was refined and practiced at Bangor as part of its history. It was returned to Europe with the monks as they ventured out on their missionary pilgrimages. Usher and Mabillon cite a tract with regard to the choral service of Bangor. The tract was called *De Cursurem Ecclesiasticorum* and there was an extant manuscript copy nine hundred years old when Usher wrote about it in 1639. The tract states:

> St. Jerome affirms that the same service [cursum] which is performed at the present time by the Scots [as the Irish were called at that time] was chanted likewise by St. Mark [the Evangelist]. Patrick, when placed by Lupus and Germanus as archbishop over the Scots [Irish] and Britons, chanted the same service there, and, after him, St. Wandilochus Senex and St. Comgall, who had about three thousand in their monastery, chanted it also. St. Wandilochus being thence sent forth as a preacher by St. Comgall, as also St. Columbanus, they arrived at Louvaine in Gaul, and there they chanted the same service, and thus that service which St. Mark the Evangelist had once chanted was revived again under the blessed Columbanus.

Usher

According to Petrie in the eighteenth century, there were Latin hymns of St. Columba (Colmcille), composed soon after the middle of the sixth century, which furnish strong reasons for believing that devine service was also chanted in concert by his monks at Iona in Scotland. Columba (Colmcille) wrote:

> May the High and Holy One
> Guard us from His Heavenly Throne,
> While we sing, with grateful hearts,
> Hymns in ten appointed parts.

"Thus it appears," wrote Petrie, "that long before the appearance of rhyme in the compositions of Continental writers, the Irish ecclesiastics of Bangor were acquainted with the choral performance of rhythmical hymns." Petrie goes on to refer to Bangor as "that illustrious school of music and theology from which the churches of Northumberland, Mercia, Germany, Franconia, Burgundy and Switzerland drew their knowledge, not only of ecclesiastical discipline and service, but of the Christian faith itself."

One of the most important surviving religious works which was produced at Bangor, is the seventh-century Bangor Antiphonary. It is now in the Ambrosian Library in Milan, Italy. The Antiphonary includes rules of worship and a creed that contains the substance of the original Nicene Creed which comes from the Council of Nicaea in Turkey in A.D. 325. Bangor's contribution to the Church is also noted in the Antiphonary:

> The holy valiant deeds
> Of sacred fathers
> Based on the matchless
> Church of Bangor;
> The noble deeds of abbots,
> Their number, time and names

Of never-ending lustre.
Hear brothers; great their deserts
Whom the Lord hath gathered
To the mansions of His Heavenly Kingdom.

4

GREEN GLENS AND BLUE HILLS

A view of Belfast's Royal Avenue. (photo provided by the Northern Ireland Tourist Board)

Belfast

The name Belfast comes from the Irish Beal Feiriste which means "The Mouth of the Sandy Ford." The small early settlement was situated on a crossing of the little River Farset, which used to run down the centre of what is now High Street, and empty into Belfast Lough. The crossing point was mentioned in the *Annals of the Four Masters* because of a battle fought there between the Ulidians and the Picts in A.D. 665.

Four monks in the early seventeenth century, three of them named O'Clery, reputedly not related, and one named O'Mulconry became known as The Four Masters. They collected all the ancient manuscripts they could find and transcribed them in Donegal Abbey into what is now called *The Annals of the Four Masters.*

The crossing on the River Farset was very well placed strategically. In the year A.D. 1177, John de Courcy built a castle between what is now Donegal Place and Corn Market to command the area from a strong position. Castle Street, Castle Lane and Castle Place all derived their names from John de Courcy's castle.

In the sixteenth century, Belfast was a fishing village and fortress in the hands of the O'Neills, earls of Tyrone. It could boast of 120 houses, a mill, a brewhouse and a partly ruined church in the beginning of the seventeenth century.

An influx of French Huguenots in 1685, brought many improvements and ideas to the already established linen industry. Linen helped to make Belfast famous throughout the world.

Belfast has always been a progressive city and in 1734, produced the world's oldest daily newspaper that still exists with its original name, the *Belfast Newsletter.* A Mr. Joy, who was an established paper maker, received a printing press in payment of a debt. Being a very smart businessman, he decided to combine his newly acquired press with his paper product and publish a daily newspaper. In 1773 the *Belfast Newsletter* published an account of a meeting in Boston called to organize the Boston Tea Party. Two weeks after the United States had issued its Declaration of Independence in 1776, the *Belfast Newsletter* published the entire text of the Declaration. It was the first newspaper in Europe to do so. The *Newsletter* got its copy from a ship's captain who had sailed into Derry, and it was rushed to Belfast for publication.

Shipbuilding was carried on in Belfast for a long time before it became world renowned as a centre for the industry. In 1636, a group of devout Presbyterians wishing to seek refuge in the New World, built themselves a 150-ton ship called *The Eagle Wing* for their journey. It was William Ritchie of Ayrshire in Scotland, who in 1791 started Belfast on its way to shipbuilding fame.

The Harland and Wolff Shipyard was started in 1858 and among the many record-breaking ships they built was the ill-fated *Titanic*. She was regarded as unsinkable. On her maiden voyage from England to New York in April 1912 she struck an iceberg, which tore a three-hundred-foot gash in her hull. The *Titanic* was the biggest ship in the world at that time. She was 882.5 feet long with a gross tonnage of 46,328. Over fifteen hundred people were lost on that calamitous night. The liner *Carpathia* picked up 705 survivors, mostly women and children.

This city has produced many noted cultural figures. Sir Samuel Ferguson, the poet and antiquarian, was born here in 1810. Canon Hannay, a novelist who wrote under the pseudonym George Birmingham, was a Belfast man. He died in 1950. John Ervine, the dramatist; poets Joseph Campbell and W. R. Rodgers; C. S. Lewis, the philosopher; and painters Sir John Lavery and Paul Henry were all from Belfast. Louis MacNeice, the twentieth-century poet was to write: "I was born in Belfast between the mountains and the gantries."

Belfast is a musical city. Its streets, homes, pubs, factories and institutions are all filled with music. The linen mills gave us songs like "The New Doffin' Mistress." Children singing in the streets contributed "I'll Tell My Ma" and "Fair Rosa," which is a street song telling the Sleeping Beauty story. Some of the well known poets have written songs. Joseph Campbell's haunting "My Lagan Love" and his beautiful "The Gartan Mother's Lullaby" are both widely regarded as very old folksongs, so well are they crafted.

The Gartan Mother's Lullaby

Sleep, O babe, for the red bee hums
The silent twilight's fall:
Aoibheall from the Grey Rock comes
To wrap the world in thrall.
O leanbhan O, my child, my joy,
My love and heart's desire,
The crickets sing you lullaby
Beside the dying fire.

Dusk is drawn, and the Green Man's Thorn
Is wreathed in rings of fog:
Siabhra sails his boat till morn
Upon the starry bog.
O leanbhan O, the paly moon
Hath brimmed her cusp in dew,
And weeps to hear the sad sleep-tune
I Sing, O love, to you.

Faintly, sweetly, the chapel bell
Rings o'er the valley dim:
Tearman's peasant voices swell
In fragrant evening hymn,
O leanbhan O, the low bell rings
My little lamb to rest,
Till night is past and morning sings
Its music in your breast.

Besides all of its own poetry and song, Belfast must always be considered a musical city because it hosted the most significant event in the history of Irish music: the great Harp Festival of 1792. A group of businessmen, calling themselves the Belfast Society in order "to revive and perpetuate the ancient music and poetry of Ireland," invited what remained of the old itinerant harpers and bards to a festival in Belfast on 11–13 July 1792. The Belfast Society, led by Dr. James McDonnell, Robert Bradshaw and Henry Joy, a son of the founder of the *Belfast Newsletter,* supplied the funding for the festival. They hired young Edward Bunting to notate and publish the music these harpers played. Bunting catalogued hundreds of pieces of music and saved for posterity a significant part of Ireland's heritage. This vast collection of ancient Irish music might otherwise have been lost for ever. It can be heard today around the world.

There were ten harpers who gathered in the large room of the Exchange Building in July 1792: Denis Hampson (97 years old) of Derry, Arthur O'Neill (58) of Tyrone, Charles Fanning (56) of Cavan, Daniel Black (75) of Derry, Charles Byrne (80) of Leitrim, Hugh Higgins (55) of Mayo, Patrick Quinn (47) and William Carr (15) both of Armagh, Rose Mooney (52) of Meath and James Duncan (45) of Down. Prizes were awarded: Charles Fanning got ten guineas, Arthur O'Neill got eight guineas and each of the rest got six guineas. Of the harpers gathered it has been said "the least able of whom has not left their like behind." These were the last of the long line of musicians and bards stretching back into the mists of antiquity. Geraldus Cambrensis, who was historian to King Henry II of England was a man well versed in arts. He described the Irish musicians of his time: "Their skill is beyond comparison, superior to any nation I have seen."

The Belfast Irish Harp Society was formed in 1807 to support a harp teacher for indigent boys. The society made tuition available to a number of boys over the age of ten from among the poor and the blind. The boys were also supplied with lodging and board. The school ran from 1807 to 1813 when it terminated "in consequence of a decline of pecuniary supplies." Arthur O'Neill, the harper and teacher at the school, continued to be paid thirty pounds a year by a few members of the society until his death.

Belfast, amidst all of its accomplishments in business and commerce, has always kept the arts very high on its agenda.

MEMORIES

I always thought that Belfast was a very commercial city. High-powered businesses, exclusive shops around the city centre and busy traffic flow with many lorries, or trucks as we call them nowadays, hauling their various commodities to and from the docks. But shining here and there through all the commerce, the arts were alive and well. What a great thrill it was for me in my youth, to see a play performed at the Group Theatre of the Arts. Stellar performances were always the norm from luminaries like Joe Tomelty, J. G. Devlin, Harold Goldblatt, Margaret D'Arcy, R. H. McCandless and the whole troup of talented theatrical people who lit up my young life. Jimmy Young was not only very funny in his shows, but thought-provoking as well.

Music and dance flourished everywhere. A young dance teacher called Patricia Mulholland combined Irish step dancing with a form of ballet and choreographed many sensational new dances like The Ardagh Chalice. She also took some of the Irish mythological legends, and with costumes designed by the Arts Department at Queen's University, created dance masterpieces. This was back in the 1950s. Patricia Mulholland's creative genius was many, many years ahead of its time. She did not receive as much acclaim as she so richly deserved.

I got my first professional acting part in Belfast. The Dublin-based Edwards, MacLiammor Company was doing a season at the Opera House. As part of that season, the legendary star Michael MacLiammor was performing in his own play *A Slipper for the Moon* and May Marrinan, an acting coach from Portadown, got me a small part with a couple of lines. It was a high point in my life to appear on that stage every night for a week, and in such august company.

My first singing performance on radio was on the BBC in Belfast. That was a live broadcast in the mid-'50s and I remember it well. I sang "Nell Flaherty's Drake" unaccompanied.

Belfast audiences are phenomenal. Another of the high points in my career was when the Clancy Brothers and I did our first Belfast concert to a capacity-packed Ulster Hall in 1963. The crowd, made up from all sections of the community, were so enthusiastic that the whole event was electrifying. Any time I've had the pleasure of performing to a Belfast audience since that night, they have been absolutely fantastic. Sometimes when I think back on Belfast in the 1960s and my mind takes a very rare excursion into the "Cynical Mode," I wonder to myself if, perhaps, someone in the shadows of power didn't like the idea of people of all creeds, classes and shades of opinion getting together and enjoying, thoroughly, a night of music and entertainment. Perhaps that person or persons, wallowing in their paranoia, decided to do something to ensure that this kind of collective enjoyment didn't go too much further.

Belfast still holds many happy memories for me, and it always will.

Lough Neagh

Lough Neagh is the largest lake in these islands being 153 square miles in area. It is bordered by counties Antrim, Armagh, Derry, Tyrone and Down. The Upper Bann River flows into the south of Lough Neagh and the Lower Bann flows from Lough Neagh out to the Atlantic. All the usual water activities are available, from pleasure boating to commercial eel fishing. In the northwest corner of the lough is the very successful Toome Eel Fisheries, which supplies the tables of mainland Europe with this delicacy.

Lough Neagh is famed in song and story. Thomas Moore, the nineteenth-century poet and songwriter, mentioned Lough Neagh in his song "Let Erin Remember":

On Lough Neagh's banks where the fisherman strays,

When the clear cold eve's declining,
He sees the round towers of other days
In the waves beneath him shining.

In the Bunting Collection of Irish music and song, one of the loveliest and strangest songs is from the shores of Lough Neagh. It is called " 'Tis Pretty to Be in Ballinderry." The song is strange in that the melody of the chorus is a harmony for the melody of the verse. It's the only song with this characteristic that Bunting found in all his years of collecting folk music.

'Tis Pretty to Be in Ballinderry

'Tis pretty to be in Ballinderry,
'Tis pretty to be in Aughalee,
'Tis prettier to be on bonny Ram's Island,
Sitting for ever beneath a tree.

    Chorus:
    Ochone, ochone, ochone, ochone!

For often I sailed to bonny Ram's Island
Arm in arm with Phelimy Diamond.
He would whistle and I would sing,
And we would make the whole island ring.

    Chorus:

I'm going, he said, from bonny Ram's Island,
Out and across the deep blue sea,
And if in your heart you love me Mary,
Open your arms at last to me.

    Chorus:

'Twas pretty to be in Ballinderry,
Now it's as sad as sad can be,
For the ship that sailed with Phelimy Diamond
Is sunk for ever beneath the sea.

Chorus:

—ANONYMOUS

The Ram's Island mentioned in the song is a small island in Lough Neagh with a forty-foot-high round tower.

Situated in southwest Lough Neagh is Coney Island. It is associated with St. Patrick and with the O'Neills, the Ulster chieftains and kings. Coney Island in Brooklyn, New York, is supposed to have been named after this little island.

There are two stories of how Lough Neagh was formed. One story is that an Irish giant and a Scottish giant were fighting. The Irish giant, in a fury, snatched a large piece of Ireland and threw it after the Scottish giant. It missed him and fell into the sea and is now known as the Isle of Man. The depression left in Ireland filled with water and is now Lough Neagh.

The other story tells of a magic well. Everyone who drew water from this well was always careful to replace the cover when they were finished. One fateful day a woman got her pitcher of water, became distracted in some way, and forgot to replace the cover. The well overflowed and a large part of the countryside became submerged. Perhaps Thomas Moore had heard this story and he mentioned the round towers beneath the waves in "Let Erin Remember."

On the shores of Lough Neagh, up in the northwest, in Arboe in County Derry, stands one of the finest high crosses in Ireland, marking an ancient monastic settlement.

Petrified wood that looks like pumice stone has been found on the shores of the lough and this fact gave us the old street rhyme:

Lough Neagh hones, Lough Neagh hones,
You put them in sticks and you take them out stones.

Antrim Coast Road and the Glens

Carrickfergus on the north shore of Belfast Lough was once a
very important port. The Norman Castle was built between A.D.
1180 and 1205. It is certainly one of the first true castles in Ireland and still very impressive. The town is also noted in song:

Carrickfergus

I wish I was in Carrickfergus,
Only for nights in Ballygrand.
I would swim over the deepest ocean,
The deepest ocean, my love to find.
But the sea is wide and I cannot swim over,
And neither have I the wings to fly,
I wish I could meet a handy boatman
To ferry me over, my love and I.

But in Kilkenny it is reported
They have marble stones there as black as ink.
With gold and silver I would support her,
But I'll sing no more 'til I get a drink.
I'm drunk today and I'm seldom sober,
A handsome rover from town to town,
Ah! but I'm sick now, my days are numbered,
Come all you young men and lay me down.

—ANONYMOUS

Passing the port of Larne, from where we could take a short
ferry ride to Stranraer in Scotland, we follow the road north and

come to the famous Antrim Coast Road. This is undoubtedly one of the most beautifully picturesque drives in Ireland. We pass through the towns of Glenarm and Carnlough. With the North Channel on our right and inland on our left we skirt the beautiful Glens of Antrim. There are nine glens whose very names are music to the ear: Glenarm, Glenariff, Glendun, Glenaan, Glen Ballyemon, Glenshesk, Glencorp, Glencloy and Glentaise.

Near the village of Waterfoot we can look seaward and glimpse the Mull of Kintyre in Scotland ten or twelve miles away. There is a story of a young man called McCambridge from Glendun. He travelled down to the sea to emigrate to Scotland. On the way down from the glen he was thinking of his friends and home and all of the things he would be leaving behind. He composed a very beautiful song in Irish. The song affected him so much that by the time he had reached the sea he had changed his mind. Turning around, he went back to his beloved glen. The song he had composed has been translated from the Irish:

The Quiet Land of Erin

By myself I'd climb the heights of Cuan
Where the mountains stand away,
And it's I would let the Sundays go,
In the Cuckoo's Glen above the bay.

> *Chorus:*
> Agus ach ach aer lighus O,
> Ar a londubh as O,
> Oh! the Quiet Land of Erin.

Oh! my heart is weary all alone,
And it sends a lonely sigh
To the land that sings beyond my dreams,
And the lonely Sundays pass me by.

I would ravel back the twisted years
In the bitter wasted wind,
If the God above would let me lie
In a quiet place above the whins.

Chorus:

Out from Cushendall, on the slopes of Tievebulliagh, is a megalithic court cairn that is regarded locally as the grave of Ossian the poet. He was the son of Finn MacCumhal, the leader of the fabled Fianna. The young poet fell in love with the very beautiful Niamh, who, with her magical powers, took him off to Tir na nOg, the land of the young. Niamh and Ossian lived in perpetual happiness, knowing only peace and joy and were never to grow old.

For a few hundred years they lived this idyllic life until Ossian was obsessed by an overpowering yearning to see Erin again and feast with the Fianna. Niamh, on acceding to his request, warned him that should he touch the earth of Erin he would take on all the years of his age and never be able to return to Tir na nOg. Ossian understood the warning but decided to return to Erin anyway. He found himself back in Erin on horseback. On enquiring for the Fianna from an old woman with a basket of turf, he discovered that the Fianna were long since gone and were now only a memory mentioned in the old stories.

While they talked, some of the turf fell from the old woman's basket. Ossian, acting instinctively on his long remembered chivalry, reached down from his horse and put the sods of turf back into the basket. Having thus touched the earth of Erin he took on all the centuries of his age. He immediately went from being a magnificent young hero to being an extremely old man and died on the spot from his great age.

We continue travelling through Cushendun and bear westward past Fair Head. This, supposedly, is the most northerly point in Ireland. We arrive in Ballycastle, where, at the Old Lamas Fair, still celebrated every August, we can, as the song says "treat our Mary Ann to Dulse and Yellow Man." Dulse is a dried seaweed, full of iodine and other minerals and vitamins. Yellow Man is a very sticky, sweet toffee.

Looking out to sea from Ballycastle we see Rathlin Island. It is an L-shaped island with about one hundred inhabitants. The contrast in colours between the white limestone and the black basalt inspired Charles Kingsley to describe it as "like a drowned magpie." It is, supposedly, here that Robert the Bruce of Scotland took refuge in a cave after his defeat at Perth in A.D. 1306.

After leaving Ballycastle, we continue westward by Ballintoy and the famous Carrick-a-rede Rope Bridge. The Bridge is eighty feet above the water. It spans a sixty-foot chasm between two points of land and is used by fishermen to net salmon whose course is through the chasm. Years ago the bridge had only one handrail, which was all the fishermen needed. When the second rail was added the fishermen considered it very decadent. Even with the two rails, it's thrilling to cross.

Close by is the Giant's Causeway, referred to locally as the Eighth Wonder of the World. In Irish it was called Clochan an Aifir (The Giant's Stepping Stones). This marvellous place was formed some 60 million years ago. Molten lava erupted through the earth's crust and in its slow cooling these polygonal columns were formed. That's what the geologists will tell you. The local people have it differently. They say that the giant Finn MacCumhal (MacCool) formed these stones so that he could get to Scotland without getting his feet wet. Strangely enough, similar columns do emerge in Staffa in Scotland.

The Giant's Causeway, known locally as the Eighth Wonder of the World. (photo provided by the Northern Ireland Tourist Board)

Causeway

Beyond the restless edges
Of the tectonic plates,
Antrim's crust is set as bone.
Beyond the fracture lines
That woke up Alp and Himalaya,
We settled and hardened
When the lava spill fulfilled
Our last assertions.
At a place east of Dunluce,
The water contorted to its touch
As the smithy's molten dip,
One hundred thousand sacred stones
Appearing out of the spasm,
Appearing out of the hollow,

Cleared at the lifting cloud.
They face towards the ocean
Like seals crowded on a shore,
They face the horizon
In their hexagonal wait,
Nor wild January, nor August quiet,
Nor tidal cover turn their head.
Century by century
The sacred things of water
Contented in their judgement.
The sacred things of fire.

—PETER MAKEM

One of the bays near the Giant's Causeway is called Port na Spaniagh where *The Girona,* one of the galleons of the Spanish Armada, foundered in A.D. 1588. In 1968 the treasure of *The Girona* was recovered and is now on display in the Ulster Museum in Belfast.

Just a couple of miles down the road from the Causeway is the village of Bushmills, home of the oldest distillery in the world. It was granted a license in 1608 and its fame has spread to the most distant places on the earth.

On the road to Portrush, stand the ruins of the magnificent Dunluce Castle. Built by Richard de Burgh, the Earl of Ulster, in A.D. 1300, this castle had a very stormy history when it was held by the McQuillan Clan. It was taken over by the Scottish McDonnells in A.D. 1560.

MEMORIES

I was driving north on the beautiful Antrim Coast Road. My lower back was a little bit sore, probably from all the driving I had been doing, but the pain was washed away by the beauty of the land and the sea on every hand. Surely, this is one of the most beautiful drives one can take. Around every bend of the road, a new vista delights the eye.

In my foolishness, I reached for the car's radio switch, expecting some wonderful music to compliment the spectacular views and to delight the ears as well. Disappointedly, I hurriedly switched from station to station on the dial and found mostly someone screaming painfully and unintelligably to a pounding bass rhythm that rattled the car's dashboard fittings. Alternatively, on one station I found Waylon Jennings singing an American country song in his own inimitable style and on the remaining station, someone was attempting to sing an American country song while trying to cover up his lovely, round-vowelled, middle-of-Ireland accent with a very questionable Texas drawl. Alas, there was no ready-made music anywhere on the radio dial that was in any way compatible with the exquisite land and sea scapes. Unfortunately this is the norm I've discovered. Since I did not have a tape player with me, I fell back on hearing, in my imagination, the singing fiddle of Sean Maguire decorating "The Mason's Apron"; the fluid fiddle elegance of Sean McLaughlin of the Glens soaring out on "Farewell to Erin"; The crystal clear voice of Mary O'Hara accompanying herself on the harp on "The Quiet Land of Erin" as only she can sing it, and my old friend, the late Arnold Elder singing "Sweet Carnlough Bay" as he did for me on many occassions. The winds blowing down from the nine green Glens of Antrim are full of music and the sea continually sings her seductive song to the blue hills. Why, oh why, can't radio music programmers listen to the land or at least to the people of the land.

Follow the North West Passage

Derry

The name Derry is an Anglicization of the Irish "Doire," which means "Place of the Oakwood." It was originally called Doire Colmcille, because in the sixth century Aimire, the Prince of Hy-Neill (The Land of the Neills), gave the area to St. Columba (Colmcille) to establish a monastery. The monastery, founded in A.D. 546, prospered and became well known. Because of its wealth, it was raided and plundered many times by the Vikings, who eventually took possession of it in the eleventh century. They fortified and held it until they were driven out in the twelfth century.

Although the Anglo-Normans never gained a foothold in Derry, the English built a fort from which to attack the powerful O'Neills in nearby Donegal. A town grew up around the fort and it was constantly under attack by the O'Neills. The town and the fort were completely destroyed in 1608.

King James I granted the ruins of the town to the City of London and they rebuilt it between 1613 and 1618 at the cost of eight thousand pounds. The famous Walls were included in the rebuilding. It was then also that the name Derry was prefixed with London.

The Derry Walls are 20 to 25 feet high and vary in width from 14 to 30 feet. Today they are the most complete fortifications of their type in Ireland or Britain. They withstood attacks in 1641 and 1649, as well as the infamous Jacobite siege in 1689.

The Jacobite siege of 1688–89 took place in December 1688 after the followers of William III, led by the governor, the Rev. George Walker, closed the gates of the city against the followers of James II, most notably the Earl of Antrim's regiment. To prevent any supplies from landing for the Williamites inside the Walls, a boom was placed across the river at present day Boom Hall. One hundred and five terrible days later the boom was broken by the ship *The Mountjoy.* Derry remained inviolate and so earned the nickname by which she is known today, "The Maiden City."

There are four gates in the Walls of Derry: The Shipquay Gate, Bishop's Gate, Butcher's Gate and Ferryquay Gate. Most of the main shopping and business streets are within the Walls. The Diamond is the centre of the city. It has four main streets, which have the same names as the Gates, running off of it.

Derry has always had more than its share of musicians and poets. The famous and lovely "Derry Air," which was originally called "Cuchullain's Farewell to Eimear," is symptomatic of Derry's musical heritage.

St. Colmcille himself was a noted poet. Because of philosophic differences with other church leaders, he left Ireland to found his famous monastery on the Isle of Iona, off the southwest coast of Scotland, with the provision that he was never again to gaze on his beloved Ireland. He wrote a poem about how he felt on leaving and it has been translated from the Irish by William Reeves and Kuno Meyer.

> There is a grey eye
> That will look back upon Erin:
> It shall never see again
> The men of Erin nor her women.

My mind is upon Erin,
Upon Loch Lene, upon Linny,
Upon the land where Ulstermen are,
Upon gentle Munster and upon Meath.

Beloved also to my heart in the west
Drumcliff on Culcinne's strand:
To gaze upon fair Loch Foyle,
The shape of its shores is delightful.

It is for this I love Derry,
For its quietness, for its purity;
All full of angels
Is every leaf on the oaks of Derry.

Were all Alba mine
From its centre to its border,
I would rather have the site of a house
In the middle of fair Derry.

A crisis arose for the bards and poets in Ireland. In A.D. 574, the Synod of Drumceatt had many complaints about the poets' abuse of their ancient privileges and was debating about whether to rescind those very extensive privileges. The bards and poets, in searching for an eloquent advocate, invited Colmcille to address the assembly on their behalf. He was brought from Iona and because of the proviso imposed on him when he left Ireland, was blindfolded as the boat got closer to the Irish shore. Still blindfolded, he was brought to Drumceatt and very eloquently and very successfully pleaded the case for his fellow poets. He concluded his address to the assembly with words that still have great significance for Ireland of today:

> . . . and for this cause, it were right for thee to buy
> the poems of the poets, and to keep the poets in Ire-

land, and since all the world is but a story, it were well for thee to buy the more enduring story, rather than the story that is less enduring.

Colcille returned to Iona with the blindfold still in place.

Derry has suffered tremendously in recent times and has had large areas of the city completely destroyed, including the magnificent Guildhall. The people of Derry, as always, have rallied to their city's aid and have gloriously restored their city completely. Derry today, is arguably the most forward looking, brightest beacon of hope and progress of any place that I know. It is a model for a troubled world to admire and follow. Slainte* Derry!

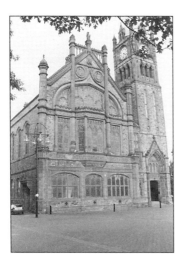

Derry's restored Guildhall sits proudly at the city's centre. (photo by Tommy Makem)

MEMORIES

I admire Derry; I admire her long musical tradition, her turn of phrase, her inbred cynical humour and her resilience.

*Slainte (pronounced slawn-che) means "Wishing you the best of everything."

Music of all descriptions has always flourished in Derry: Irish traditional music, song and dance, classical music, choral music, Dixieland jazz, progressive pop, country music and rock-n-roll. Each generation produces an abundance of artistic talent.

I have visited Derry during some of her bad times when she had not only been devastated by economic neglect and decay culminating in the closing of factories, but had literally been pummeled into rubble by military and paramilitary alike. It is notable that the Ghandi- and Martin Luther King–inspired civil rights marches originated in Derry in 1969. Her music and humour helped her survive those terrible times. Derry's sons and daughters with vision, ability, entrepreneurial spirit and drive have rebuilt and rejuvenated their city. The music and humour still shine through. A friend from Derry and I were discussing a mutual friend who is very brilliant and a bit "off the wall" as they say, and my Derry friend described him very well: "His head is full of wee doors and they're all banging."

It's hard not to like a place that produces thinking like that so I frequently visit and enjoy the Derry of today.

The Grianan of Aileach

As we take the road that runs from Derry towards Letterkenny, in County Donegal, ten or twelve miles out, on the left-hand side, we come to a very beautiful, very modern circular church. On a wall leading up to the church door, we find a number of sun signs, among them, the Aztec Indian sun sign. Looking up from where we are to the top of an eight-hundred-foot-high hill at Carrowreagh, we can see the Grianan of Aileach, the Sun Palace of Aileach.

This circular stone temple, measuring 77 feet in diameter, has 17.5-foot-high walls that average about 13 feet in thickness at the base, and was built to worship the Sun-God in 1700 B.C. It was built around the same era as Thebes in Greece and before

Solomon had built his temple in Jerusalem. The walls are terraced on the inside and two passages run through them from near the entrance. Commanding magnificent views of Lough Foyle on one side, and Lough Swilly on the other, the Grianan completely dominates the Inishowen Peninsula. The great Ulster chieftains, O'Neil, the Earl of Tyrone and O'Donnell, the Earl of Tirconnell, sailed out of Lough Swilly to the Continent in 1607 in what is known as the Flight of the Earls.

The Grianan of Aileach was taken over in the fourth century by Niall of the Nine Hostages, who was the forebear of the O'Neills. It became a stronghold of the O'Neill's, kings of Ulster and was occupied until the twelfth century.

Restored between 1874 and 1878, the Grianan of Aileach remains in all its glory to remind us vividly of Ireland's massive cultural heritage.

It's a very mystical place, where you can almost hear on the wind, the words of the poet Ossian: "A tale of the times of old—the deeds of the days of other years."

A view of the circular stone walls of the Grianan of Aileach, the Sun Palace of Aileach. (photo provided by Irish Tourist Board)

MEMORIES

On a bright May morning we approached the impressive Grianan of Aileach to do a television interview with my friend Roy Arbuckle. As the crew set up their cameras and sophisticated sound equipment, Roy was chuckling away to himself. I asked him to let me in on the joke, too. He said "They're doing all this work for nothing. They'll never be able to record anything inside these walls." I couldn't understand why not and neither could the crew. They had enough battery power to run both the cameras and the sound equipment for at least two hours of recording.

We started the interview and in less than a minute Charlie Ebel the sound engineer called "Hold it! There's something happening with my metres." Charlie adjusted whatever needed adjusting and, thinking everything was working properly we started again. The metres on Charlie's recorder started acting up again. This went on for about an hour and a half. Eventually through fits and starts we got the fifteen minute interview finished and all the batteries went dead! We were all nonplussed by these strange happenings inside the walls of the Grianan of Aileach.

Roy seemed to understand the workings of some hidden forces in this magical place. He was chuckling all the way back into Derry.

Ardara

Patrick MacGill, who was born in Donegal in 1890 and was affectionately called "the Navvy Poet," wrote in praise of his people in his poem "Dedication":

> I speak with a proud tongue of the people who
>   were
> And the people who are

The worthy of Ardara, the Rosses and Inishkeel,
My kindred—
The people of the hills and the dark-haired passes,
My neighbours on the lift of the brae,*
In the lap of the valley,
To them Slainte!

Travelling southwest from Letterkenny through beautiful, ever-changing County Donegal, through the town of Glenties, we eventually come to Ardara. This is the home of Donegal homespun tweeds. All of the beautiful colours of the local flora and fauna are artfully woven into the wonderful fabric and its colours, texture, wearability and generally handsome look that have made it a household name.

Ardara, which means "Height of the Ringfort," is situated on a peninsula between Loughros Mor Bay and its sister Loughros Beg Bay. The trout and salmon fishing are excellent here. Not far from the town, the Maghera Caves, the lovely Essaranka Waterfall and the Slievetooey Mountains, bound by the Atlantic Ocean, are all interesting and scenically excellent.

MEMORIES

I remember when making a little film for television some years ago, I spent ten days in an hotel in a certain town in County Donegal. The hotel was very comfortable, the staff friendly, and the food excellent. The one problem was that for dinner every evening the potatoes were always "chips" or, as some call them "french fries." The locals who ate at the hotel seemed to prefer these, I suppose because they usually had boiled potatoes at home when they ate there. I, on the other hand, would much prefer to have the lovely boiled potatoes.

About the sixth or seventh night of my stay when going into the din-

*A *brae* is a small hill.

ing room I was approached by a very embarrassed manager who apologised profusely because the chip machine had broken down and I would have to make do with boiled potatoes in their jackets or mashed.

I had definitely not prayed for this to happen, but God is good anyway.

Glencolmbkille

Out on the southwest coast of Donegal and just north of Slieve League, there is a beautiful, wild, warm, secluded glen. This is Glencolmbkille. It was a retreat for St. Colmcille, or as he was also known, St. Columba. Natives will be glad to point out St. Colmcille's Bed or his Oratory. There is an engraved stone in the Oratory, and the shrine is still a place of pilgrimage. Local folklore has it that Charles Edward Stuart (Bonny Prince Charlie) spent some time here.

Emigration was taking a heavy toll at Glencolmbkille. The powers that be in Dublin seemed to have forgotten about this distant, lonely area. A local priest, Father McDyer, decided he was going to do something about the situation and being wise as he was, knew that God would help those who help themselves. Father McDyer planned, organized and founded a unique co-operative movement. With the help and backing of the people of the glen and indeed students and general helpers from all over Ireland and Continental Europe, the movement installed a water and sewage system and rural electrification.

They started home industries, helped farmers, learned to market all that they produced, built houses and generally turned around the economy of the area. Glencolmbkille was booming and becoming a model for many areas throughout the country. Now, along with all the other accomplishments of the Clencolmbkille Co-Operative, there is a folk village with cottages representing three different periods in Irish rural life. I believe one can rent a cottage and spend a very relaxing week or two in these most peaceful surroundings and with very warm, welcoming people. To Glencolmbkille, too, Slainte.

Killybegs

Killybegs is noted for sail-making and for hand-knotted carpets. Some Killybegs carpets grace Buckingham Palace. Most of all, Killybegs is known for its fishing fleet. Situated on Donegal Bay, Killybegs Harbour is a very busy place, which can boast of its own fish-processing plant.

It seems that a native son called Paddy Gallagher went off to work in Scotland, like thousands of other Donegal people before him. While working there, Paddy became very interested in the way that the local Scottish people had organized themselves into a smooth running, self-help co-operative, colloquially called "the Co-Op." On returning to Killybegs, he found that, amongst other things, the local fishermen were looking for a solution about what to do with the excess fish they had taken. Paddy, with his experience of how the people in Scotland solved a lot of their local problems organized the good people of Killybegs into a co-operative of their own, and the fish-processing plant is one of the results.

The word *co-operative,* of course, became shortened to co-op, and that in time became "the Cope." Because of his ideas and efforts in organizing the co-operative movement, Paddy Gallagher became, and is still fondly remembered as, "Paddy the Cope."

I wrote a song some years ago about the Killybegs fishermen:

The Boys of Killybegs

There are wild and rocky hills on the coast of
   Donegal

And her fishermen are hardy, brave and free,
And the big Atlantic swell is a thing I know right
   well
As they fight to take a living from the sea.

Chorus:
With a pleasant rolling sea, and the herring run-
ning free
And the fleet all riding gently through the foam,
When the boats are loaded down, there'll be
singing in the town,
When the Boys of Killybegs come rolling home.

Now you don your rubber boots, and you've got
   your oilskins on
And you check your gear to see that it's okay,
And your jumper keeps you warm, for it's cold be-
   fore the dawn
Then you're ready to begin another day.

Chorus:

When the wind is blowing rough, then the work is
   very tough,
And the ropes will raise the welts upon your
   hand.
But whoever you may be, you will never leave the
   sea,
When it's in your blood, it's hard to live on land.

Chorus:

Now you're headed out to sea, and the wind is
   blowing free,

And you cast your nets as rain begins to fall,
But the sun comes riding high and the clouds will
    soon roll by,
And today you'll maybe take a bumper haul.

Chorus:

There is purple on the hills and there's green
    down by the shore,
And the sun has spilled his gold upon the sea,
And there's silver down below, where the herring
    fishes go,
When we catch them, we'll have gold for you and
    me.

Chorus:

In the wall of the Catholic Church in Killybegs, there is a sculptured slab commemorating Niall Mor MacSweeney, a MacSweeney clan chieftain. This is one of only two slabs of this kind. The other slab is in Creeslough, County Donegal. It also commemorates a MacSweeney chieftain.

Lough Erne

Lough Erne, in County Fermanagh, is one of the scenic splendours of Ireland. It has fifty miles of navigable water and is dotted with some 154 islands. This is a fisherman's paradise with roach, bream, pike, gudgeon, eels and rudd all lining up, waiting to be caught.

Some of the islands are extremely interesting. For instance, there is the ruin of a twelfth-century church on White Island on lower Lough Erne that has eight very mysterious carved stone figures. The figures were found at various times between 1840 and 1958 and had seemingly been buried or hidden for some obscure reason. No one seems to know much about the origins of the figures or the reason for their existence, and they are a strange assortment. One of the figures is obviously an ecclesiastic carrying a crozier and a bell. Another is the pagan female fertility goddess Sheila na Gig. I would guess, and it's only a guess, that the figures may be from the sixth century, when Christianity was replacing paganism and was using some of the symbols of the pagan gods and goddesses to achieve the takeover.

On Boa Island, which is linked to the mainland by bridges, we find two very ancient and very interesting stones. Each stone forms two figures back to back. Some people see the stone, not as two separate figures, but as one figure with two faces. This is probably the Celtic/pagan version of the Roman god Janus, who was seeing both life and death. The mystique of the ancient Celts is usually based in duality. All their mysteries and ceremonies took place at dawn or twilight, when it was neither day, nor night, or in the mist, which is neither air nor water. They held mistletoe to be sacred or mystical because it was neither tree nor bush, so Janus, with the two faces must have been a very popular and highly worshipped god.

On Devinish Island, there are the ruins of a monastery founded by St. Molaise between A.D. 564 and 571. It was an Augustinian monastery called St. Mary's Abbey. Directly beside it is a very well-preserved round tower dating from the tenth to the twelfth century. The tower, which is eighty-one-feet high, has a finely carved cornice of faces with the beards and moustaches all intertwining.

These eight mysterious stones are among the ruins of a twelfth-century church on White Island. (photo by Tommy Makem)

Enniskillen

The town of Enniskillen occupies a very strategic position on the neck of land between Upper and Lower Lough Erne. It is a very pleasant, business-like marketing centre. A lovely winding main street has different names in various parts of the street. The sight of waters of either the Lough or the River Erne pops into view all over the town.

One of the more important buildings in Enniskillen is St. MacCartan's Cathedral. It was built on top of one of the town's hills about 1841. On another hill is Portora Royal School, which can boast of having had both Oscar Wilde and Samuel Beckett as students.

In the fifteenth century Hugh Maguire, who was known as "Hugh the Hospitable," built a castle here. A Captain Cole, in the seventeenth century, added to it. The County and the Regimental Museums are housed there now.

The county had two notable British Army regiments—The Royal Inniskilling Fusiliers and The Inniskilling Dragoons. There was an old song about the Dragoons that had obscure verses and a very singable chorus. I wrote new verses to it and retained the old chorus. You will notice the difference in spelling in my version.

Fare Thee Well Enniskillen

Our troop was made ready at the dawn of the day,
From lovely Enniskillen they were marching us
    away,
They put us then on board a ship to cross the raging main,
To fight in bloody battle in the sunny land of
    Spain.

Chorus:
Fare thee well Enniskillen, fare thee well for a
while,
And all around the borders of Erin's green isle,
And when the war is over we'll return in full
bloom
And you'll all welcome home your Enniskillen
Dragoons.

Oh! Spain it is a gallant land where wine and ale
    flow free;
There's lots of lovely women there to dandle on
    your knee,
And often in a tavern there we'd make the rafters
    ring
When every soldier in the house would raise his
    glass and sing.

Chorus:

We fought for Ireland's glory there and many a
      man did fall,
From musket and from bayonet and from thun-
      dering cannonball,
And many a foeman we laid low amid the battle
      throng,
And as we prepared for action you would often
      hear this song.

Chorus:

Well now the fighting's over and for home we have
      set sail.
Our flag above this lofty ship is fluttering in the
      gale.
They've given us a pension, boys, of fourpence
      each a day,
And when we reach Enniskillen, never more we'll
      have to say.

Chorus:

Omagh

Omagh is the county town of County Tyrone. It stands on a hill
overlooking where the Camowen and the Drumragh Rivers
meet to form the River Strule. For generations it has been a garrison town.

   Two important hills on the northwest horizon are Bessy Bell
and Mary Gray. The two got their names from the family of the
Duke of Abercorn whose home is near Baron's Court Forest
Park. On the summit of Bessy Bell there are magnificent views

of The Sperrin Mountains, Lough Erne to the west and County Donegal to the northwest.

A few miles north of Omagh the Ulster American Folk Park has grown up around the ancestral home of the Mellon family. Thomas Mellon emigrated from here to Pennsylvania in 1818. He founded a dynasty, including the Mellon Bank, in the Pittsburgh area. The Folk Park has houses and craft workshops showing how the emigrants lived in the Old World and houses from America showing the type of living conditions they found in the New World.

Out at Gortin, which was Gaelic speaking up until within living memory, a splendid new Heritage Park has been opened. It portrays life in Ireland from prehistoric man up to the seventeenth century. It's a wonderful achievement.

> I've tramped through Derry and the County Kerry
> And Portaferry in the County Down,
> But in all my raking and undertaking,
> My heart was aching for sweet Omagh town.

> —ANONYMOUS

6

YEATS COUNTRY

Poets and Fiddlers

One day a few years ago I remember driving from Enniskillen to Sligo. Passing through Glencar on the eastern side of Ben Bulben, there is a spectacular view of a waterfall that tumbles from the flat top of the mountain to the valley 1,722 feet below. On this particular day there was a tremendously strong updraft of wind from the valley that actually blew the water back up to the top again. It was a very strange sight.

On the Dublin Road a few miles out of Sligo town is Drumcliff and its famous churchyard where William Butler Yeats, the poet, is buried.

St. Colmcille founded a monastery here in A.D. 574 and there is a fine high cross to mark the spot.

Although Yeats was not born in Sligo, he started coming here as a boy with his parents who were both Sligonians. He wrote a number of poems about Sligo, including the very popular "Lake Isle of Innisfree." In nearby Ballisodare, Yeats supposedly heard someone sing a very beautiful traditional song called "The Rambling Boys of Pleasure." He was delighted by the song. On returning to where he was staying, he started to write down what he remembered of the Rambling Boys. Discovering that he had only the feeling of the song, he wrote one of his own based on the old one he had heard. Yeats called his composition "An Old Song Re-Sung." It eventually became known as "Down by the Sally Gardens."

Down by the Sally Gardens

Down by the Sally Gardens my love and I did
  meet.
She passed the Sally Gardens with little snow-
  white feet.
She bade me take love easy as the leaves grow on
  the tree,
But I being young and foolish, with her did not
  agree.

In a field by the river my love and I did stand,
And on my leaning shoulder she placed her snow-
  white hand.
She bade me take life easy as the grass grows on
  the weirs,
But I was young and foolish and now I am full of
  tears.

William Butler Yeats died in France in 1939. His body was taken home at his own request and reinterred in Drumcliff where his grandfather had once been rector. The inscription on his gravestone reads:

Cast a cold eye
On life, on death.
Horseman, pass by.

There is a Yeats School held here every summer and scholars come from all over the world to participate.

North of Drumcliff Bay is Lissadell House, home of the Gore Booth family, where Yeats was a frequent visitor. Lisadell House was built in the 1830s with local Ballisodare limestone. It has a unique music room with concealed lighting and perfect acoustics. In the dining room, there are life-size murals of the domestic staff which were painted by the Polish Count Markievicz. He had married Constance Gore Booth. She is remembered for her involvement in the 1916 rebellion in Dublin.

County Sligo is the birthplace of some of the most important and influential Irish traditional fiddlers. The best known were Michael Coleman, James Morrison and Paddy Killoran. They played so distinctively that their style, often copied, has become known as Sligo-style fiddling. The tradition lives on.

MEMORIES

I was visiting Yeats's gravesite on a late spring afternoon when a coach full of tourists arrived. One older lady was reading the inscription on the headstone. Her friend asked her what it said. She read aloud: "Cast a cold eye on life, on death. Horseman, pass by." The friend exclaimed "Is that all?!"

There was a lettered plate lying loose on the white quartz chippings on the grave, explaining that George Yeats was also buried there. An older man who seemed to be a little hard of hearing asked a younger man beside him "Who was George Yeats?" The younger man replied "George was his wife." To which the older man said "Oh well—as long as they were happy!!"

On that note, I passed by. Some days are diamonds.

Carrowkeel, Co. Sligo

In Carrowkeel, which is about two miles northwest of the village of Ballinafad in County Sligo, there is a cemetery of megalithic passage graves. Of the sixteen tombs on the site, thirteen are passage graves, while two of the three remaining are cist burial mounds. The last one has features of both a court cairn grave and a passage grave. This mixture of features is evidence of the influence of two different cultures. In 1911, the site was excavated and there were many archaeological "finds," including pottery that was so distinctive in style that it is now called Carrowkeel pottery. Among the other discoveries were bone pins, stoneheads and pendants, all dating back to the Neolithic or late Stone Age, at least 3000 B.C.

Near the burial complex there are fifty stone rings referred to as "The Village." Some people believe that these are the remains of the houses or shelters used by the tomb builders.

Boyle

The town of Boyle in County Roscommon is situated at the foot of the Curlew Mountains between Lough Gara and Lough Key. Boyle Abbey is a very well preserved Cistercian abbey which was founded in 1161. It was colonized by monks from Mellifont Abbey in County Louth.

A couple of miles west of Boyle, we find the Drumanone Portal Grave, which is one of the largest in Ireland.

In 1952, during draining operations on the shores of Lough Gara, about 350 or 360 lake dwellings, or crannogs as they are called, were discovered. In the years that followed, a number of these crannogs were excavated by a Dr. Raftery, who found many prehistoric relics. More and more artifacts were discovered as the lake level fell, including a number of bronze instruments, forty dug-out boats and many fishing instruments from the late Mesolithic and early Neolithic ages. These excavations showed that the area around Boyle had been inhabited continuously from at least 3000 B.C. until about A.D. 500.

Keadue, Co. Roscommon

During the late seventeenth and early eighteenth century, Turlough O'Carolan, the last and most famous of the Irish bards, lived here in Keadue, Co. Roscommon. He was a harper, composer and poet, and was considered a great genius.

O'Carolan was born in Nobber, Co. Meath, in 1670. Like many in his profession, he was blind, losing his sight to smallpox. He was a man of very deep and very versatile talents and was prolific in his artistic accomplishments. One of the harpers, who played at the Harp Festival in Belfast in 1792, and who had never met O'Carolan, played about one hundred of O'Carolan's compositions, and said that this constituted but a very small portion of O'Carolan's music. Indeed, I have read somewhere, that at the Belfast Harp Festival, two hundred tunes were attributed to O'Carolan, and these were the ones that the harpers had remembered. I don't know if any of these numbers are true or not, but I certainly read them somewhere.

At the house of an Irish nobleman, the Italian violinist and composer Geminiani was present and O'Carolan challenged him to a test of skills. Geminiani played the Fifth Concerto of Vivaldi. O'Carolan immediately played it back note for note, although he had never heard it before. He surprised the gathering even more, when he said he could compose a concerto himself, and picking up his harp, played the piece that has since been known as O'Carolan's Concerto.

According to a close friend of his, he composed his music using the buttons on his coat to represent the lines and spaces of the music staff.

O'Carolan's music lives on very vibrantly, thanks to the Belfast Harp Festival of 1792 and the work of the collector Edward Bunting.

Some of his poetry has also been handed on to us. In a tribute to one of his patrons, Keane O'Hara, O'Carolan wrote "The

Cup of O'Hara," which has been translated from the Irish by
Sir Samuel Ferguson.

The Cup of O'Hara

Were I in Green Arran
Or south in Glanmore,
Where the long ships come laden
With claret in store;
Yet I'd rather than shiploads
Of claret, and ships,
Have your white cup, O'Hara,
Up full at my lips.

But why seek in numbers
It's virtue to tell,
When O'Hara's own chaplain
Has said, saying well—
Turlough, son of Brian,
Sit ye down, boy, again,
Till we drain the great cupaun*
In another health to Keane.

O'Carolan died in 1738 and is buried in the Old Church of
Kilronan on the shores of Lough Meelagh. His name and
achievements are celebrated with a music festival in his honour in Keadue every summer.

Cupaun is probably a colloquialism for cup.

7

CRUACHAIN OF THE POETS

Rathcroghan

This mound between Frenchpark and Tulsk, here in County Roscommon, is 204 feet in diameter and is one of the very special places in Ireland. It was from here that the legendary Queen Maeve, with her husband King Ailill, ruled her province of Connacht. Queen Maeve was, undoubtedly, one of the most romantic, colourful and impressive figures in ancient Ireland. It was Maeve who gave Cruachain, as it was called then, the splendour for which it was renowned. After the magnificent Emhain Macha in Ulster, Cruachain is the next most important place in the earliest known Irish literature.

It was here that Maeve gathered her armies and led them to Cooley, on the shores of Carlingford Lough, in what is now County Louth. Cooley, at that time, was the southeast corner of Ulster. Maeve's army set out to capture and take back to Cruachain for herself, the Brown Bull of Cooley. This Brown Bull of Cooley was the only beast in Ireland superior to her husband Ailill's White Bull of Connacht. So, Maeve, beautiful, flamboyant, headstrong, intelligent and powerful, became one of the principal players in Irish literature's greatest epic, *"An Tain Bo Cualigne"*—"The Cattle Raid of Cooley."

Lady Gregory, in her wonderful book *Cuchullain of Muirthemne* describes the palace at Cruachain like this:

> "This now was the appearance of Cruachain, the Royal House of Ailill and of Maeve, that some called Cruachain of the Poets; there were seven divisions in the house, with couches in them, from the hearth of the wall; a front of bronze to every division, and of red yew with carvings on it; and there were seven strips of bronze from the foundation to the roof of the house. The house was made of oak, and the roof was covered with oak shingles; sixteen windows with glass there were and shutters of bronze on them, and a bar of bronze across every shutter. There was a raised place in the middle of the house for Ailill and Maeve, with silver fronts and strips of bronze around it, and four bronze pillars on it, and a silver rod beside it, the way Ailill and Maeve could strike the middle beam and check their people.
>
> And outside the royal house was the dun [hill fort] with the walls about it that were built by Brocc, son of Blar, and the great gate; and it is there the houses were for strangers to be lodged."

In Glenballythomas, about a half-mile southwest from here, there is a limestone cave known as the Cave of Cruacha, an entrance to the Otherworld.

Queen Maeve will never be forgotten as long as this hill stands and *An Tain Bo Cualigne* remains as a vivid memorial to her in the hearts and minds of all in this land.

The buildings may be gone from Cruachain, this storied hill, but the magic still remains.

Ballyhaunis

In 1348, Jordan Duff MacCostello built an Augustinian friary in Ballyhaunis, Co. Mayo. In need of repair, it was rebuilt in 1641. Nine or ten years later, around 1650, Oliver Cromwell's troops burned it. The remains of it were restored in 1938.

Two and a half miles west of the town is the Bracklaghboy Ogham Stone, which stands in Lisvaun. It is six feet high and stands in a circular mound, which is twenty-one feet in diameter.

Ogham was an early form of writing, with markings on either side of a perpendicular line, forming the letters.

Sean O'Boyle, the late Gaelic scholar and musicologist believed that Ogham writing was originally very ancient musical notation and some other scholars agree with him. Whatever its origin, Ogham stones may be found all over the country, and they are a very strong link to a very ancient heritage.

Ballina

Ballina stands sentry over where the River Moy empties in Killala Bay. It is a natural centre for the excellent fishing that is so popular throughout the north of County Mayo.

In the town of Ballina, we find the ruins of an Augustinian monastery that was built in 1427.

On the road to Lough Conn, about a half a mile south of the town, the Dolmen of the Four Maols has a story to tell. It seems that in the sixth century, there were four foster brothers, who murdered their tutor Ceallach, who happened to be the bishop of Kilmore-Moy. I don't know why they were driven to murder him, but the bishop's brother hanged the four in Ardnaree on the other side of the river. The dolmen marks the grave, or graves of the four foster brothers.

During the rebellion of 1798, the Irish patriots in Mayo got a little help from the French in the form of eleven hundred soldiers under the command of General Humbert. They landed in Killala on 22 August and took the town. Proceeding to Ballina, they took that also before heading west to Castlebar. The landing and battles are recounted in a well known song.

The Men of the West

When you honour in song and in story,
The names of the patriot men,
Where valour has covered in glory,
Full many a mountain and glen.
Forget not the boys of the heather
Where rallied our bravest and best,
When Ireland lay broken in Wexford
And looked for revenge to the west.

> *Chorus:*
> I give you the gallant old west, boys,
> Where rallied our bravest and best
> When Ireland lay broken and bleeding
> Hurrah! for the men of the west.

The hilltops with glory were glowing,
'Twas the eve of a bright harvest day,
When the ships we'd been wearily 'waiting
Sailed into Killala's broad bay.
And over the hills went the slogan
To waken in every breast
The fire that has never been quenched, boys,
Among the true hearts of the west.

> *Chorus:*

Killala was ours ere the midnight
And high over Ballina town,
Our banners in triumph were waving,
Before the next sun had gone down.
We gathered to speed the good work, boys,
The true men anear and afar,
And history can tell you we routed
The redcoats, through old Castlebar.

Chorus:

I pledge you the stout sons of France, boys,
Bold Humbert and all his brave men,
Whose march in the red field of battle
Brought hope to our hearts once again.
And Connacht is ready whenever
The loud rolling beat of the drum,
Rings out to announce the good news, boys,
And tell us the morning has come.

Chorus:

—WILLIAM ROONEY

Ceide Fields

A year or two ago, if an archaeologist was asked how a Stone
Age farmer lived, he would have said that Neolithic man would
have cleared a small area in the forest in which to plant his
crops. Out along the beautiful wild coast of north Mayo, past
Killala and its eighty-four-foot round tower; past the well-
preserved cloisters and tower of Moyne Abbey, which were
built in 1460; past Ballycastle and out towards Downpatrick
Head lies Ceide, where they have set that archaeological the-

ory on its ear. Under six feet of peat they have discovered Stone Age farms laid out exactly as farms are laid out all over Ireland to the present day: small fields bounded by stone fences with dwellings here and there and looking as rural Ireland does right now. All of this has been dated back to the late Stone Age, five thousand years ago. There is a new Interpretive Centre at Ceide Fields. It's a large glass pyramid rising up gloriously from the bogs and staring out to sea. The centre is carefully planned, with all kinds of information and exhibits explaining what life around Ceide must have been like from 3000 B.C. to the present.

Nearby the Ceide Fields is Downpatrick Head. Standing about one hundred feet out in the water is a large rock. The rock is the same height and was, undoubtedly, the point of the headland at one time. The story of how it split from the Head is a wonderful piece of local folklore.

Crom Cruach, who was one of the pre-Christian gods, resided on the headland and kept a fire burning continually. He dominated the whole area and everyone feared him. St. Patrick was travelling in the area and approached the point of the headland. Crom Cruach rose up against him. The saint picked up a rock, carved a cross on it, lifted it with both hands above his head and roaring out a prayer, hurled the rock with great force into the fire. There was a mighty explosion and a blinding flash. When the smoke and confusion cleared, the point of the headland had split off and was sitting out in the water with Crom Cruach still on it. He was destined to remain there until he died, which wasn't too long afterwards. According to the story he suffered horribly, being eaten to death by midges.

MEMORIES

Ceide is the same name as my home-town on the eastern side of Ireland, Keady in County Armagh.

While visiting Ceide Fields in County Mayo to tape some material for a television show, the crew had set up the camera and the sound recording equipment. The sound engineer had turned on his machine to record some atmospherics. Suddenly he put his hands up to his earphones and got a startled look on his face. "That's very strange. I don't believe this!" He handed me the earphones and said "Listen to this." Putting on the earphones I heard what seemed like the woodwind section of an orchestra playing lovely minor chords that kept changing. We couldn't figure it out. Was it the telephone wires humming? Remember as a child, putting your ear to the telephone pole to hear the sound? Was it some errant radio waves? Perhaps sound waves from a television satellite dish? Maybe it was ghost sounds already on the tape? It was none of these. I went over to stand at a gate in the hedge to think about the origins of these strange sounds and discovered that the sounds were coming from the gate.

It was a normal five-barred gate made from tubular metal. There were a couple of little air holes in each bar of the gate to release any moisture that might accumulate in the tubing. The wind blowing through these holes was playing a mellifluous five-note minor chord that kept changing with the ups and downs of the wind.

So much for the mysterious music! The engineer taped some of the sounds and they will make a lovely mellow background for the visual shots of this ancient place.

Westport

Westport was a very important town before the heyday of railways. The river was made into a canal, and quays and bridges were built during the eighteenth century. Agricultural produce was exported from here. Timber from the Baltics and America; manufactured goods from Britain as well as many other commodities were imported through here. Westport is now a thriving fishing centre.

Canon Hannay, who wrote novels under the pseudonym of George A. Birmingham, was rector here for many years. W. M. Thackeray while visiting Westport in 1842, described the scenery around Clew Bay as "the most beautiful in the world."

Newport

Here, where the Newport River flows into Clew Bay, stands the town of Newport. It's a very fine angling centre surrounded by picturesque drumlins, long narrow hills, which are not only pleasant to look at, but are of geological interest as well.

On the shores of Clew Bay, about three miles west of here, the Burke family built a castle in the sixteenth century. It was called Carrigahooley Castle, but is known nowadays as Rockfleet.

One of the Burkes of Carrigahooley Castle married the wild, exotic pirate queen Grania O'Malley. She led her own fleet of ships out of Clew Bay and swashbuckled her way not only into history, but into the hearts of the people of Ireland. She withstood a seige here in 1574, and took up residence in 1583.

Queen Elizabeth I of England, one of the most powerful women in history, if not afraid of Grania, at least held her in deep respect. The story is told that Grania, after being invited to meet Elizabeth, arrived at the castle, dressed, not in attire in keeping with a royal visit, but in her seafaring clothes, swords and all. Striding, with head held high, up to the queen on her throne, Grania announced "I'm Grania O'Malley." Elizabeth said "You didn't bow to me," to which Grania replied "I bow to no one."

There are many stories about the exploits of Grania O'Malley, both true and untrue. One story tells of a time when she stopped at a nobleman's manor and after being kept waiting for some time, became very irritated by the discourtesy. After sending one of the man's children to ask why she was being kept waiting so long, the man sent the child back to tell her that he was dining and would see her when he was finished. Taking this as an insult and a grave breach of the rules of hospitality, Grania kidnapped the child, and held him for two weeks. She then returned the child, unharmed, with the stipulation that from that time forth, the family would always set an extra place at their table for any visitor who might stop by their door. Up to the present time, that family is said to honour the edict and set an extra place at their table, at every meal.

Grania O'Malley attacked a prison where her husband was being held. She overcame the guards, released her husband and took him home. Later on, when Grania herself had been captured, and was being held in prison, for piracy, I suppose, Queen Elizabeth had her pardoned and released out of regard for her.

The people of Ireland still delight in the pirate queen, Grania O'Malley.

Croagh Patrick

Rising twenty-five hundred feet above the south shore of Clew Bay, Croagh Patrick is a place of pilgrimage. It all goes back to the year A.D. 441, when St. Patrick fasted and prayed for forty days atop the mountain. On the last Sunday in July, locally called Garland Sunday, pilgrims come from all over the country to climb the mountain and pray. Many of the pilgrims climb the mountain barefoot. It is a very tough climb, even wearing shoes, but climbing over the small stones and quartzite rubble on bare feet is severe penance indeed. The climb to the top of Croagh Patrick begins at the lovely fourteenth-century Augustinian monastery, Murrisk Abbey.

Legend has it, that it was here during his forty-day pilgrimage, St. Patrick banished all the venomous snakes from Ireland.

Lough na Corra, near the southern base of the mountain is

said to have burst forth when St. Patrick threw a terrible demon called Corra from the summit of the holy mountain.

The splendid remains of twelfth-century Cong Abbey. (photo provided by the Irish Tourist Board)

Cong

The picturesque village of Cong in County Mayo has an early monastic tradition. St. Fechin of Fore founded a monastery here in the sixth century, but only one small piece remains of that original abbey. The present abbey remains are of an Augustinian monastery founded in the twelfth century by King Turloch O'Conor. The cross in the middle of the village is erected on the base of a medieval cross.

Ashford Castle, once the home of the Guinness family, is now a luxury hotel, magnificently located on the shores of Lough Corrib. In the early 1950s, the film *The Quiet Man* was shot in and around this lovely village.

For me, Cong's claim to fame is due to the fact that just northeast of the village lies the ancient plain of South Moytura. This is where the First Battle of Moytura was fought.

The Firbolgs inhabited and ruled Ireland about 1400 B.C., when the magical, mystical Tuatha De Danaan, the followers of the Goddess Dana, made their first appearance in Ireland, here at Cong. The De Danaans, according to mythology, came from four great cities of magic in the Otherworld; Falias, Gorias, Finias and Murias. They had learned science, craftsmanship and the magical arts from four great sages, each one a ruler of one of the four cities. According to the *Book of Invasions,* when the De Danaans came to Ireland, they took with them a gift from each of the four cities. From Falias, they took a great stone called the Lia Fail, the Stone of Destiny, on which the high kings of Ireland were crowned. The people knew they had a rightful monarch when, on the king being crowned, the stone roared.

The actual stone used for the inauguration, existed at the Royal Hill of Tara in County Meath, until it was sent to Scotland early in the sixth century. A man called Fergus Mac Erc was to be crowned king of Scotland and he asked his brother Murtagh Mac Erc, who was king of Ireland, for the loan of the stone for his coronation. The Lia Fail became the famous Stone of Scone. It never came back to Ireland, but was removed to England in A.D. 1297 by King Edward I. It is now the Coronation Stone in Westminster Abbey. There was later a prophecy connected to the Lia Fail that stated that wherever the Stone of Destiny was, a monarch of Irish-Milesian race should reign. The old prophecy has not proven false. According to T. W. Rolleston's wonderful book *Celtic,* the British Royal family can be traced back to the historic Milesian kings of Ireland through Fergus Mac Erc and the Stuarts.

The other gifts the De Danaans brought to Ireland were the invincible sword of Lugh of the Long Hand, the Celtic Sun God, which came from Gorias; a magic spear from Finias; and the Cauldron of the Dagda from Murias. The Cauldron of the

Dagda could feed a great host of people and still remain full.

The Tuatha De Danaan had fortified a camp and the Firbolgs sent an emissary called Sreng to find out all he could about these strangers. The De Danaan sent their emissary Bres to meet Sreng. They examined each others' spears and weapons. The spears of the De Danaan were light and extremely sharp, and the weapons of the Firbolgs were heavy, blunt and awkward to handle. Here were the forces of light and knowledge, the De Danaans and the forces of darkness and brute force, the Firbolgs. The De Danaans proposed that the two races should divide the country between them and guard it against all enemies, but the Firbolgs at first, were not convinced of the De Danaan superiority and refused their offer.

On thinking over the situation, they came to the conclusion that the De Danaan must be necromancers to be able to make such magical weapons and that perhaps they were too hasty in deciding to do battle. They had decided, and battle was inevitable. But perhaps, they could delay the inevitable. The Firbolgs used many excuses to delay the fatal encounter. Firstly, they needed time to have light spears made like the ones of the De Danaan, then they had to sharpen their swords. More time was needed to put their spears in order and finally, time was essential to furbish their armour and their helmets. All this delay and scheming kept the De Danaan fretting and impatient for 105 days before the battle finally started. The De Danaan gained some points also. The Firbolg had a much larger number of warriors and the laws of battle dictated that both sides had to fight on equal terms, warrior for warrior. The Firbolg had to reduce their numbers.

The battle lasted for four days and the De Danaan were victorious. The Firbolg's King Eochaid was slain and they noted that Sreng, their great champion had maimed King Nuada of the De Danaan by cutting off his hand. This caused Nuada to lose the kingship because under De Danaan law, no king could rule who had a personal blemish. The De Danaan chief artificer Creidne later made a new hand out of silver and attached it to Nuada's arm, once again leaving him without a blemish. He was known ever after as Nuada of the Silver Hand. The De Danaan won the Battle of South Moytura because of their superiority in all the sciences, including healing. The Firbolg, according to T. W. Rolleston, were probably a veritable historic race. Their conflict with the De Danaan may be a piece of actual history invested with some of the features of a myth.

So, this plain at Cong is a very special place because the magical, mystical De Danaan chose it to make their first appearance in Ireland.

The County of Mayo

On the deck of Paddy Lynch's boat I sat in woeful
    plight,
With my sighing all the weary day and weeping all
    the night.
Were it not that full of sorrow from my people
    forth I go,
By the Blessed Son 'tis royally I'd sing thy praise
    Mayo.

When I dwelt at home in plenty, and my gold did
    much abound,
In the company of fair young maids the Spanish
    ale went round,
'Tis a bitter change from those gay days that now
    I'm forced to go,
And must leave my bones in Santa Cruz, far from
    my own Mayo.

They are altered girls in Irrul now; 'tis proud
    they're grown and high,
With their hair-bags and their top-knots, for I pass
    their buckles by,

But it's little now I heed their airs, for God will
    have it so,
That I must depart for foreign lands and leave my
    sweet Mayo.

'Tis my grief that Paddy Loughlin is not Earl of
    Irrul still,
And that Brian Duff no longer rules as lord upon
    the hill,
Or that Colonel Hugh McGrady should be lying
    dead and low,
And I sailing, sailing swiftly, from the County of
    Mayo.

—ANONYMOUS

8

CONNEMARA AND OTHER DELIGHTS

Clifden

The town of Clifden, on the northern end of Clifden Bay, is the capital of Connemara. Noted for the beauty of its landscape, Connemara is also famous for the small, hardy Connemara pony and the distinctive, speckled, olive green Connemara marble.

With a backdrop of a spectacular range of mountains, called the Twelve Pins, the highest of which is Benbaun at twenty-four hundred feet, Clifden is a thriving market town. It is blessed with sandy coves and strands within a mile of the town. About four miles away, White Strand in Derrygimla, and Leguan and Mannin beaches, not much farther on, are very popular bathing sites.

In 1919 Alcock and Brown landed here at the end of the first transatlantic flight. A monument in the shape of a vertical tail fin of an aircraft, marks the spot near Mannin where they landed.

Clifden Castle was built by the D'Arcy Clan in 1815.

Connemara, wild and very beautiful, is a place not to be missed.

MEMORIES

On my way to Connemara recently, I stopped in Spiddal to say hello to my old friends the Standuns. I had to stand back and admire the magnificent building that houses their international business enterprise.

Many years ago I remember spending many nights very happily in the Standuns' house making music with the family and neighbours until the morning sun had warmed the road. Great music it was, too.

The Standuns at that time had a building beside the dwelling house where some local women knitted Aran sweaters and worked at other local crafts while Martin and Mrs. Standun, and indeed the children when they became able to do it, worked at all kinds of jobs to get their business going. They prospered and grew through their very hard work and good sense into the wonderful enterprise they are today. Long may they prosper.

I bought my first Aran sweater from the Standuns all those many, many years ago. Their graciousness and hospitality have not diminished since those long-ago days, nor their love of the music. Even today, any time I come anywhere near the Standuns' establishment I know there is great music floating around in the Spiddal air.

Pedestrians stroll along pleasant William Street, one of many in the walkable city of Galway. (photo provided by the Irish Tourist Board)

Galway

Galway city, here on the shores of the lovely Galway Bay, is the gateway to Connemara. It's a warm, friendly city and for me one of the most pleasantly walkable places I know. The very air seems sweet, gentle, deep-rooted and Gaelic. Ruled by the Burke Clan at one time, the city was taken over by fourteen English families who held it until 1654. Because of these fourteen tribes, the city has ever since been called "The City of the Tribes."

In 1588 the Spanish Armada, coming in by a northern route, was caught in tremendous storms and its ships wrecked, many off the coast of Galway. Many of the survivors settled in the area and to this day there is a definite Spanish influence about the city. One of the landmarks here in Galway is the Spanish Arch, the site of an old fish market.

The area known as The Claddagh was a very traditional enclave. It is now lined with new houses. The area gave its name to the Claddagh Ring. This ring has two hands holding a heart, topped by a crown. The heart represents love, the hands friendship and the crown loyalty. There are two ways to wear the ring. If it is worn with the crown pointed towards the arm, it means that the wearer's heart is free to be given. However, if the ring is worn with the crown pointed towards the fingertips, it means that the wearer's heart is already in the keeping of another.

The story is told of a young man from Galway who had emigrated to Spain. Whilst there he was apprenticed to a goldsmith. He became a famous goldsmith himself and designed the ring with the hands, heart and crown for a Spanish nobleman. On returning to his native Galway, his ring became very popular for marriages in The Claddagh area. In recent years its popularity has spread world wide.

There is a bank in Shop Street occupying what was Lynch's Castle. In 1493, the Mayor of Galway was James Lynch

Fitzstephen, a wine importer. The son of a business friend from Cadiz in Spain was staying with him as a guest. This young man's name was Gomez. Walter Lynch, the mayor's son suspected the young Gomez of trying to steal his girlfriend and he murdered him. Walter was charged with the murder and was brought up before his father who was also a magistrate. The father found his son guilty and ordered him to be hanged. No one could be found to carry out the hanging sentence and Walter was held in jail. On receiving information that a mob of Walter's friends planned to break into the prison and free him, the judge hanged his own son from a window of the castle. That incident, supposedly, is where the term "Lynch Law" originated.

Galway is a lovely city. One may wander its streets and see street musicians everywhere. Stake a claim to a place in one of its many wonderful pubs and while away the evening, surrounded by good music, humour, stimulating conversation and always convivial company. Good restaurants abound serving excellent food, many of them specializing in local seafood.

At the right time of year, stand on Salmon Weir Bridge, as countless thousands have done and watch the multitudes of salmon as they travel upriver to spawn.

There is a Gaelic theatre here called The Taidhbhearc, which specializes in plays in the Irish language.

Galway has festivals and special activities all year 'round. Near the top of the list is the highly sociable Oyster Festival in September. Patrons may not only partake of the succulent Galway Bay oysters, washed down with pints of Guinness, but dance and carouse the night and indeed the days away. One may also take part in such activities as the Oyster Opening Championship.

In August, one of the great social events in the country takes place with the Galway Races, famed high and low all over Ireland.

The Galway Races

As I roved out through Galway town, to seek for
    recreation,
On the 17th of August, my mind being elevated,
There were multitudes assembled with their tickets
    at the station,
My eyes began to dazzle and I going to see the races.

Chorus:
With me whack fol the doe fol the diddley I dil day

There were multitudes from Aran, and members
    from New Quay Shore,
The boys from Connemara and the Clare unmar-
    ried maidens.
There were people from Cork city who were loyal
    true and faithful,
They brought home the Fenian prisoners from
    dying in foreign nations.

Chorus:

It's there you'll see confectioners, with sugar sticks
    and dainties,
With lozenges, and oranges, and lemonade, and
    raisins.
The gingerbread and spices to accomodate the
    ladies,
And a big crubeen* for tuppence to be picking
    while you're able.

Chorus:

*A *crubeen* is a pig's foot.

It's there you'll see the pipers and the fiddlers
  competing,
The nimble-footed dancers and they tripping on
  the daisies.
There were others crying "Cigars and lights, and
  bills for all the races,
With the colours of the jockeys, and the prize and
  horses' ages."

Chorus:

It's there you'll see the jockeys and they mounted
  on so stately,
The blue, the pink, the red and green, the emblem
  of our nation.
When the bell was rung for starting all the horses
  seemed impatient,
I thought they never stood on ground, their speed
  was so amazing.

Chorus:

There was half a million people there of all de-
  nominations,
The Catholic, the Protestant, the Jew and Presby-
  terian,
There was yet no animosity, no matter what per-
  suasion,
But failte* and hospitality inducing fresh acquaintance.

Chorus:

—ANONYMOUS

*Failte means welcome.

MEMORIES

When you say the word crack, *or as some spell it* craic, *in Ireland, everyone knows that you are referring to fun, gaiety, music, good times, dancing, laughter, good conversation and general hilarity, or a combination of any or all of these. The word has absolutely nothing in common with the iniquitous drug, crack cocaine.*

On an American coach tour of Ireland in which I was travelling, we had pulled into Galway to overnight in an hotel there. Everyone set out to enjoy all the many fine diversions that Galway has to offer. Taking a very pleasant walk, I met two of the ladies from the tour who seemed to be quite upset. I enquired the cause of their agitation. One of the women explained that they had been in a certain pub thoroughly enjoying the music and the acquaintance and friendship of what both of them considered "a most likeable, friendly, well-mannered, happy young couple." During the general enjoyment, the young man of this happy couple suggested that the four of them should move to another establishment just down the street where, as he put it, "they have far better crack." My two friends from the tour told me in no uncertain terms, as I'm sure they told this young couple, that they would not be caught next or near any place where illegal drugs were available. So saying, they took off at a hot pace.

Later, back at the hotel when I explained the situation to them they were very embarrassed, but laughed hilariously at their mistake and wondered what that young couple must think of them!

Clonmacnoise, County Offaly

In A.D. 548, Dermot McCarroll gave land to St. Ciaran, to found a monastery in Clonmacnoise. Three Kingdoms, Connacht, Munster and Meath, met here. Dermot McCarroll was later to become High King Dermot. St. Ciaran's monastery flourished and grew in wealth and influence and was destined to become one of the most celebrated ecclesiastical sites in the country. Being prosperous, the monastery was plundered many times by marauders, including the Vikings. The most famous Viking raid took place in A.D. 844, when Turgesius, accompanied by his wife Ota, sailed up the Shannon River and plundered and burned the monastery.

The ruins in Clonmacnoise include a cathedral, a castle, eight churches, five high crosses (two only partial), two round towers and two hundred monumental slabs.

The North Cross was erected in the ninth century, but only the shaft remains. It is the oldest cross in Clonmacnoise. The cathedral, a simple sixty-two-foot rectangle, was built in A.D. 904, but very little of the original building still exists. In the tenth century, King Flann's Cross, or the Cross of the Scriptures, as it's also known, was erected near the west door of the cathedral. It is richly decorated with scenes of the Crucifixion and the Last Judgement. It has animal figures around its base. The South Cross, which dates from the eleventh century, also depicts the Crucifixion. The Nuns Church, built by Queen Dervorgilla in A.D. 1167, has a beautiful Irish Romanesque chancel arch still surviving.

The last high king of Ireland, Rory O'Connor, was buried in Clonmacnoise in A.D. 1198.

A British army garrison, stationed in Athlone, wrecked the cathedral in A.D. 1552 and its restoration in 1647 was short lived as Oliver Cromwell's soldiers destroyed it once again in the 1650s.

Angus O'Gillan, a fourteenth-century poet, wrote of the dead of Clonmacnoise, and T. W. Rolleston translated his poem from the Irish:

The Dead at Clonmacnoise

In a quiet water'd land, a land of roses, stands St.
    Kieran's city fair:
And the warriors of Erin in their famous genera-
    tions slumber there.
There beneath the dewy hillside sleep the noblest
    of the Clan of Conn,
Each below his stone with name in branching
    Ogham and the sacred knot thereon.

There they laid to rest the seven Kings of Tara,
There the sons of Cairbre sleep—
Battle-banners of the Gael, that in Kiernan's plain
    of crosses
Now their final hosting keep.

And in Clonmacnoise they laid the men of Teffia,
And right many a lord of Breagh;
Deep the sod above Clan Creide and Clan Conaill,
Kind in hall and fierce in fray.

Many and many a son of Conn, the Hundred
    Fighter,
In the red earth lies at rest;
Many a blue eye of Clan Colman the turf covers,
Many a swan white breast.

9

WHERE MUSIC FLOWS

The Burren, County Clare

The hauntingly lonely area known as the Burren, in County Clare, is fifty square miles of bare limestone terraces and rocks. Strangely enough, there are many exotic flowers and plants growing here. Rare orchids, many not found anywhere else, saxifrages and gentians grow in profusion. Many Alpine and Arctic types abound, and they grow everywhere from the highest reaches down to sea level. There is a spectacular view of the Burren from Corkscrew Hill, which as the name suggests, is an extremely twisty, hilly road between Ballyvaughan and Lisdoonvarna.

In the town of Lisdoonvarna, they have a very enjoyable match-making festival every year. Visitors attend from all over the world. Of course, County Clare in general, and the village of Doolan in particular, are renowned as deep havens of Irish traditional instrumental music. They are also famous for their dances, like the Clare Sets, and their accomplished and enthusiastic dancers.

The whole area of the Burren has many antiquities. Dolmens, wedge gallery graves, forts and crosses dot the land. The four-thousand-year-old Poulnabrone Dolmen is arguably, the most photographed dolmen in Ireland. Seven miles northeast of Kilfenora, is found a stone tomb called the Druid's Altar.

Slieve Elva at 1,134 feet is the highest elevation on the Burren. Along its flank, there are seven miles of caverns known as the Polnagollum caves system. Many of the streams on this starkly beautiful area, disappear into potholes and caves, after they have crossed from the shale of the higher elevations to the limestone farther down. Pot-holing, more commonly known as spelunking in the States, is popular in the area. I wonder if, perhaps, J.R.R. Tolkien knew of Polnagollum when he was writing his fantastic *Lord of the Rings.*

Bunratty Castle

Bunratty Castle, in County Clare, is on the road from Shannon Airport to Limerick. It was built by Sioda MacConmara in the mid-fifteenth century. By the year A.D. 1500, it had become the home of the O'Briens, kings of Thomond, themselves descendants of King Brian Boru. A castle has stood on this site since around A.D. 1250. Oliver Cromwell's army besieged the castle in A.D. 1650.

In the 1950s, Lord Gort restored the castle and refurbished it, very impressively, with furniture, utensils, weapons and tapestries from the fifteenth and sixteenth centuries.

There is a very colourful folk park attached to Bunratty Castle that contains cottages, houses and businesses from the area, all authentically furnished and fitted out. It's a very interesting and lovely place to visit, just for its own sake and is a wonderful place to spend some time while waiting to go in to the medieval banquet in the castle.

Nowadays, Bunratty Castle hosts many thousands of visitors

every year at its medieval banquets. It was the first place to host these feasts in modern times. Many places all over the world have followed its lead, but for me and countless others, Bunratty remains the best in its field. It's a very enjoyable experience and I recommend it to any tourist. Be sure to make reservations, because it's extremely popular.

Memories

Fiddles, flutes, concertinas, pipes, accordians, bodhrans, dancing feet, laughter, singing, occassional bursts of exuberant cheering—space to sit down, as scarce as fat on a greyhound—men, women and children, funeral-slow traffic on the outskirts of town, a hotel manager making futile attempts to stop the music at 2 A.M., finally, after very prolonged efforts achieving enough silence to speak and in that first split second of silence, being asked to sing a bar of a song himself and resignedly, and with great good humour, rendering "Fare Thee Well Enniskillen" beautifully, and to thunderous applause. A fresh-faced young man, his fair hair in a pony tail, before long hair was popular, being asked by a well-fortified farmer if he'd care to dance; a fiddler asleep stretched out on a shelf in a shop window; music everywhere, in pubs, shops, private houses, alleyways, back yards, gardens, graveyards, doorways, street corners, music! music! music! A joyous throng revelling in the magnificence of their own culture, sending it resounding around the world.

This was the Fleadh Ceoil (Music Festival) in Ennis in the early 1960s. I can still savour it any time I'm in County Clare.

The Treaty Stone with King John's Castle in the background. (photo by Tommy Makem)

Limerick

With its busy port and with Shannon International Airport only thirteen miles away, Limerick is a very important market, industrial and communications centre. The town itself, was built by the Vikings in the early tenth century, as a centre from which they could pillage and plunder the area. They continued their raiding for a century until they were driven out by the king of Thomond and his brother, the famous Brian Boru. Many of the Norsemen settled down here and were allowed to function as traders. Limerick became the seat of the O'Brien kings.

The siege by the English king William III in 1690 is arguably the greatest historical and traumatic event in Limerick's annals. King James II had left the French general Lauzun in charge of the Irish forces in Limerick. Lauzan, in a very arrogant gesture, declared that the walls of the city could be knocked down with roasted apples and immediately took off for Galway. The governor of Limerick and Patrick Sarsfield had to take over the defense of the city. King William III brought twenty-six thousand troops before the walls of Limerick in August 1690. His artillery was to follow from Cashel in County Tipperary. Patrick Sarsfield took a troop of horse soldiers out to Ballyneety. They defeated William's artillery and forced him to abandon his siege by the end of August.

In the following year, William sent the very experienced and accomplished Ginkel to start a strong siege of the city. He attempted to enter the city through breeches in the walls, but was repelled. Ginkel then made a very vigorous drive on the Thomond Bridge defenses and inflicted very heavy losses on the defenders. The people of Limerick were under extreme pressure at this time and waiting for promised relief, which never came. The city negotiated a surrender to Ginkel. The gallant Sarsfield left the city at the head of ten thousand troops and embarked for France. It was the first exile of native aristocracy since the Flight of the Earls O'Neill and O'Donnell in 1607. The leaving of Sarsfield and his followers became known as "The Flight of the Wild Geese."

The terms of the treaty were not honoured by the English. The Treaty Stone on which the Treaty of Limerick is supposed to have been signed, has ever since been called "The Stone of the Violated Treaty."

The Jackets Green

When I was a maiden fair and young,
On the pleasant banks of Lee,
No bird that in the greenwood sung
Was half so blithe and free.
My heart ne'er beat with flying feet
No love sang me his queen,

Till down the Glen rode Sarsfield's men,
And they wore the jackets green.

Young Donal sat on his gallant grey
Like a king on a royal seat,
And my heart leaped out on his regal way
To worship at his feet.
Oh, love, had you come in those colours dressed,
And wooed with a soldier's mien,
I'd have laid my head on your throbbing breast,
For the sake of your jacket green.

When William stormed with shot and shell
At the walls of Garryowen,
In the breach of death my Donal fell
And he sleeps near the Treaty Stone.
That breach the foemen never crossed
While he swung his broadsword keen;
But I do not weep my darling lost
For he fell in his jacket green.

I saw the Shannon's purple tide
Roll by the Irish town,
As I stood in the breach by Donal's side
When England's flag went down.
And now it lowers when I see the skies,
Like a blood-red curse between.
I weep, but 'tis not women's sighs
Will raise our Irish green.

Oh, Ireland, sad is the lonely soul,
And loud beats the winter sea,
But sadder and higher the wild waves roll
O'er the hearts that break for thee.
Yet grief will come to our heartless foes,
And their thones in the dust be seen,

So, Irish maids, love none but those
Who wear the jackets green.

—MICHAEL SCANLAN

Lough Gur

On the Tipperary road running to the east of Limerick, we find Lough Gur. Situated near Sixmilebridge, Lough Gur is the centre of one of the most important prehistoric sites in Ireland.

In the nineteenth century, the Lough was drained, bringing the water to its present level. During the drainage, several lake dwellings or crannogs were discovered. Numerous objects that may have been thrown in the water as votive offerings were also found. These objects or "finds" were to provide a large portion of the information we have on Neolithic and Bronze Age man in Ireland today.

Along the shores of Lough Gur, there is an early Christian earthen ring fort. This consists of a group of hut sites called "The Spectacles." Because of the way that they are joined together, they look like a pair of eyeglasses. They date to the fifth or sixth century A.D.

There are two stone forts, probably built by the Vikings, on Carraigh Aille and they are known as Carraigh Aille I and II. Among many "finds" during excavations were several tons of animal bones, which help archaeologists to date the forts to between the eighth and tenth century A.D.

Also in the area, is Bourchier's Castle, which dates to the fifteenth century A.D. and is very well preserved. An early Bronze Age tomb has been discovered. Remains of some species of animals now extinct in Ireland, such as giant Irish deer and bear have been found in caves in the hills above the lake.

Perhaps the two most striking and important features in the Lough Gur complex, are the two stone circles. One of these is considered the largest stone circle in Ireland, measuring about 150 feet in diameter. The stones, placed edge to edge, are very large, the largest being fourteen feet high, with an additional five feet under the ground. The interior of the circle was filled up with clay, to level it out and also to hide the packing stones at the base of the upright standing stones. This clay has yielded many "finds," including beaker type pottery (which dates it to the Bronze Age), flints, stone axes and even some bronze objects.

From the numerous finds in the Lough Gur area, it is possible to show a continuous settlement by man from 3000 B.C.

One of the thatched cottages with its lovely flower garden for which the village of Adare is known and loved. (photo by Tommy Makem)

Adare, County Limerick

Adare is situated about ten miles from Limerick City on the way to Killarney. It is one of the most picturesque villages to be found in Ireland. The beautifully kept thatched cottages, with their very colourful flower gardens, create a distinctive Old World atmosphere.

This is the home of the earls of Dunraven, who can trace their ancestry back to a third century A.D. king of Munster. The second earl of Dunraven built a magnificent neo-Gothic mansion called Adare Manor. The manor, which was started in 1832, is now a luxury hotel in immaculately manicured grounds, and boasting beautiful gardens and stately old trees.

Near the village, stands a thirteenth-century Trinitarian abbey and an early Augustinian abbey. They have been partially restored by the Dunravens for the two religious communities in the village. In the Augustinian abbey, a carved Tudor rose is reputed to be the only one in the Republic. There are also the ruins of a fifteenth-century Franciscan monastery and a thirteenth-century castle, which was built by the O'Donovans.

The Limerick Rake

I am an old rake that is hardy and bold,
In Castletownconners I'm very well known,
In Newcastlewest I spent many a note
With Kitty and Judy and Mary.
My father rebuked me for being such a rake,
And for spending my time in such frolicsome
    ways,
But I ne'er could forget the good nature of Jane;
Agus fagaimid siud mar ata se.*

*The English translation of this Irish phrase is "That's enough said about it."

My parents they taught me to rake and to mow,
To plow and to harrow, to reap and to sow,
But my heart being too airy to step it so low,
I set out on a high speculation.
On paper and parchment they taught me to write,
In Euclid and grammar in troth I was bright,
But in multiplication I opened their eyes;
Agus fagaimid siud mar ata se.

If I chance for to go to the market of Croom,
With a cock in my hat, and my pipes in full tune,
I'm welcomed at once and brought up to a room,
Where Bacchus is sporting with Venus.
There's Peggy and Jane from the town of Bruree,
And Biddy from Bruff and we all on a spree,
Such a combing of locks as there was about me;
Agus fagaimid siud mar ata se.

If I chance for to go to the town of Rathkeal,
The girls all around me do flock on the square,
Some give me a bottle, and others sweet cakes,
To treat me annonced to their fathers.
There's one from Askeaton, and one from the
    Pike,
And another from Ardagh my heart has beguiled,
Though being from the mountains her stockings
    are white;
Agus fagaimid siud mar ata se.

To quarrel for riches I ne'er was inclined
For the greatest of misers must leave them be-
    hind,
I'll purchase a cow that will never run dry
And I'll milk her by twisting her horn.
John Damer of Shronel had plenty of gold,

And Devonshire's treasure was twenty times more,
But they're laid on their backs amongst nettles and
     stones;
Agus fagaimid siud mar ata se.

This cow can be milked without clover or grass,
For she's pampered with corn, good barley and
     hops,
She's warm and she's stout and she's free in her
     paps,
And she'll milk without spancel or halter.
The man that will drink it will cock his caubeen,*
And if anyone laughs there'll be wigs on the green,
And the feeble old hag will get supple and free;
Agus fagaimid siud mar ata se.

There's some say I'm foolish and more say I'm
     wise,
Being fond of the women, I think it's no crime,
For the son of King David had ten hundred wives,
And his wisdom was highly regarded.
I'll till a good garden and live at my ease,
And each woman and child can partake of the
     same,
If there's war in the cabin themselves they may
     blame;
Agus fagaimid siud mar ata se.

And now for the future, I mean to be wise,
I'll send for the women who acted so kind,
And I'll marry them all on the morrow by 'n' by,
If the clergy agree to the bargain.
When I'm on my back and my soul is at rest,

Caubeen is Irish for hat.

These women will crowd for to cry at my wake,
And their sons and their daughters will offer a
    prayer
To the Lord for the soul of their father.

—ANONYMOUS

10

THE KINGDOM OF KERRY

Tralee, Ardfert and Mount Brandon

Tralee, the gateway to the magnificent Dingle Peninsula, is the county town of County Kerry. It is a very pleasant, well laid out, vigorous modern business centre.

Every year, Tralee celebrates the very successful Rose of Tralee Festival, with contestants from all over the world.

The Siamsa Theatre, a traditional Irish folk theatre incorporating song, dance and local folklore, is headquartered here.

Tralee was home to the earls of Desmond. Their principal castle was situated where the elegant Georgian houses of Denny Street meet The Mall. The walls of the limestone Ionic Courthouse, built by Sir Richard Morrison, still stand, but the roof, unfortunately, is missing.

The modern church of Our Lady and St. Brendan is shaped like a wide-bodied currach or canoe in tribute to St. Brendan the Navigator.

St. Brendan was born the son of Findlug, in Annagh, on Tralee Bay in A.D. 484. It is said that when she was pregnant with Brendan, his mother had a dream that her bosom was filled with pure gold. As was the custom at that time, when Brendan was a year old, he was given into fosterage to a nun called Ita, who raised him until he was five. At the age of five,

Brendan went to study with the local Bishop Erc, who taught him the canon of both the Old and the New Testament. Brendan became a monk and later established a number of monasteries, among them Clonfert in County Galway and Ardfert, about five miles northwest of Tralee, where he also built a cathedral. The remains of the cathedral that are standing in Ardfert now are those of a thirteenth-century cathedral, built on the site of St. Brendan's original sixth-century one.

He got his name, Brendan the Navigator, because of his travels, which took him not only to many parts of Ireland, but to Wales, England and France, or Gaul as it was called then. He also travelled as far as the Canary Islands, which were then called the Fortunate Isles.

Further voyages took him to the Island of Iona, off the southwest coast of Scotland, to visit St. Colmcille. His major voyage, however, was his epic voyage to the west, in which it is believed he landed in what is now North America, back in the sixth century. He wrote the *Navigatio Brendani* on this voyage and over one hundred copies in Latin are extant. It has also been translated into English. At one point during this momentous voyage, his boat reached Iceland, where a few of his monks stayed, established monasteries, and brought Christianity to that country.

Continuing his voyage, he saw many wonders and experienced many adventures, including seeing icebergs, whales and many other strange things he had never seen before. He finally made landfall in Newfoundland in Eastern Canada. Resting for some time in Newfoundland, he started out once more and sailed down the east coast of Canada and the United States. He stopped in a number of places, including what is now St. Augustine, in Florida, before returning to Ireland. On pre-Columbian maps, what was known as "St. Brendan's Country" was just south of the Antilles and west of the Cape Verde Islands.

Travelling out from Tralee to the Dingle Peninsula, we come upon Mt. Brandan, which was named for the saint. He had his retreat at the summit. A path from the village of Cloghane climbs to a lip of the mountain and meets up with a zigzag path, that reaches to the top of the mountain. The path was made by thousands of pilgrims, who have climbed to visit Brendan's cell, oratory and well.

It is said that it was at Brandon Creek that St. Brendan and his monks built and fashioned their boat from tanned cowhides, lashed together with leather thongs. They set off from here on their voyage to the west to find the "Land of Promise."

In 1977, Tim Severin, a young adventurer, built a replica of Brendan's boat and crossed the Atlantic to North America, much as St. Brendan did in the sixth century, proving that it could have been done. National Geographic did a major spread in their magazine and a television show on Tim Severin's voyage, retracing Brendan's journey. The cowhide boat that Severin used for his voyage is on display at Craggaunowen in County Clare.

After his voyage to North America, Brendan returned to Ireland and continued his work with the monasteries he had founded. He died in Ardfert in A.D. 577.

Brendan

Our masts and keel were made of oak,
We had cowhide all around,
She was fitted right, she was water tight,
And we were outward bound.
Our sails were white in the morning light,
The Celtic Cross our sign,
By Brendan blessed, we were headed west,
And the land fell far behind.

Chorus:
Brendan, holy Brendan,
He sailed uncharted waters, he discovered lands
    unknown.
Brendan, holy Brendan,
He was a saintly sailor, and he steered us safely
    home.

We'd a favouring wind for weeks on end
And we could take our ease,
One cloudy morn it suddenly turned
And brought us mount'nous seas.
Between the waves was darkened caves,
But Brendan brought us through,
He roared a prayer that the Lord might spare
Our ship and all her crew.

Chorus:

We saw strange sights, both days and nights,
And Brendan wrote them down;
Fish that fly, and a rainbowed sky,
And a floating crystal town,
And a giant thing that could swim and sing,
Blew water through its head,
A fish that talked and on water walked,
And a crew that was damn near dead.

Chorus:

We had nearly died when Brendan cried
There is landfall near at hand,
An albatross our bow has crossed,
And we're approaching land.
We ran aground on the land, new found,
And we rested many days.
Spirits were good, fresh water and food,
We all sang Brendan's praise.

Chorus:

It was turning cold, and it might take hold,
We headed out once more.
We were southward bound, and the only sound
Was the wind and the water's roar.

We had no storm and the sun grew warm,
We once again made land,
With fruits to eat, all fresh and sweet,
A paradise for man.

Chorus:

Now we're home again through the wind and rain,
And homeland hills look green,
And Brendan's charts map out the parts
Where no one else had been.
Now winter nights by the firelight,
I live it all again,
How a saintly man with a prayer and a plan,
Had charted the western main.

Chorus:

—TOMMY MAKEM

MEMORIES

I was visiting inlaws in the Listowel area, and rising a little early in the morning I went for a walk.

It was a beautiful April morning, sparkling, fresh with dew and sunshine. The birds seemed to be in particularly good voice and I was feeling very bright and happy as I stepped it out, whistling in answer to them. After walking about a mile I decided to turn back as thoughts of a nice cup of tea kept trifling with my taste buds. Exchanging "good mornings" with some people who were delivering milk to a tanker truck, I was retracing my steps when I sensed a car driving behind me at the same pace as my walk. Being a little suspicious, I dodged over to a gate to have a look at the river at the bottom of the field, by the way, but also to let the car move ahead. The car stopped and my old friend Sean McCarthy emerged, to my delight. A neighbour of his had been giving him a lift into town.

When Sean recognised me from the car, he decided to walk with me as I was going in the direction of Listowel.

We were having a great chat and Sean was pointing out the places of interest to me, this being his home territory. "Do you see that fine big farm over there?" says he. "I was hired there when I was a lump of a lad. One morning I was driving a herd of cows from the house there, to a field farther along the road. After closing the gate behind the cows I took a notion to keep travelling. Eventually I ended up in London. It was seven or eight years before I got back home again. After getting off the bus in Listowel I was walking out the road towards home and on passing the field where I had left the cattle I saw that there was a herd in that same field. I opened the gate, drove the cows up to the farm, walked into the kitchen and asked the woman of the house if the grub was ready. Being the decent woman she was, she laughed like hell, thanked me for taking the cattle home, even if they were a little late, and made me a grand feed."

He shook hands with me, saying "I've got to go, I have urgent business in Listowel. By God, I'm delighted to see you!" Off he went, laughing at the fond memory of taking the cows home somewhat late.

Kerry is like that. Time was made for enjoying in this wonderful place.

The Dingle Peninsula

The town of Dingle was a fort site long before the Normans came. Its busy port did a very prosperous trade, especially with Spain. It is still a very charming, essentially Irish town and the Irish language is used extensively throughout the area. Dingle has been called the next parish to America.

A few miles northwest of Dingle on an unclassified road near Smerwick Harbour, stands Gallarus Oratory. It is generally believed to date from the sixth century. The oratory, which measures 22 feet long by 18 feet wide and stands 16 feet high, is built of stone. No mortar of any kind had been used in the construction. The stones are so perfectly fitted together, that no water has penetrated the building in twelve hundred years.

Gallarus Oratory, which is shaped like a very deep boat set upside down, is widely regarded as the most perfectly preserved early Christian church building in the country.

The road from Dingle, via Slea Head to Ventry, is not only magnificently beautiful, but has large numbers of prehistoric and early Christian sites. Along the road approaching Slea Head, there are numerous small, round, stone buildings called Beehive Huts. They were built, according to local folklore, by early Christian monks. Whoever built them certainly picked a magnificent site. The view of the Blasket Islands is superb. The road right around Slea Head and all the way to Ventry is stunningly beautiful. Between Ventry and Dingle Bays, there is a jut of land, which is supposed to be the last place in Ireland where the Vikings lived as a distinct and separate people.

The stunning site of Slea Head. (photo by Tommy Makem)

MEMORIES

A friend of mine was adjudicating at a music festival in southwest County Kerry. After finishing his work judging the competitions, he had adjourned to one of the very crowded pubs to have a pint before the 11.30 P.M. closing time. The music and the "crack" were revved up, and elbowing his way to the bar he got his pint. Having finished it at about 11.25 he ordered another one which he was sipping slowly. The jollification around him, as they say, was immense. Looking at his watch he realised it was after midnight and the music and singing were showing no signs of abating nor the doors of being closed. Chancing his arm, he ordered another pint and was promptly served by the proprietor. Around 2 A.M. he was about to leave, the music and laughter and noise still in full swing, when out of curiosity he said to the proprietor "I think this is great, but aren't you supposed to close at half past eleven?" To which the proprietor replied laughingly "Well we tried that early closing when it came out first, but it didn't catch on at all."

Killorglin, County Kerry

Every August, the good people of Killorglin are busy finishing the preparations for what has become one of the major events in the Irish social calendar, Puck Fair. The young people of the town, I'm told, go out into the mountains and capture a wild male goat and bring him back alive to the town. Meanwhile, other people have erected a high platform and the goat, bedecked with colourful ribbons, is crowned king of the fair and hoisted up to the top. He reigns as King Puck over the three-day festival.

This fertility festival has been celebrated joyously year after year since pagan times. It has, amongst other activities, a cattle, horse and sheep fair. The first day of the festival on 10 August is called Gathering Day, the second Puck Fair Day, and the third, Scattering Day. In keeping with the non-stop celebration, normal closing times in the town are suspended for the duration of the festival. Thousands of people from all over the world throng to Killorglin for these ancient and unique festivities.

Cahirciveen, County Kerry

Cahirciveen, on the Ring of Kerry, is known as the birthplace of Daniel O'Connell. He was called The Liberator because of his tremendous work in bringing about Catholic Emancipation in Ireland against strong opposition in the British Parliament. The charismatic O'Connell was born in Carhan House in Cahirciveen in 1775.

A few miles west of Cahirciveen is Valentia Island, named by the Spanish. The first successful transatlantic telegraph cable was completed between North America and Ireland, here at Valentia Island in 1866.

Nearby is massive Leacanabuaile Fort. During excavations in 1939, quernstones and bone combs were discovered that date the fort to at least early Christian occupation.

A monastery until the twelfth century, the Skelligs are now home to thousands of sea birds. (photo provided by the Irish Tourist Board)

The Skelligs Rocks

Lying eight miles to the southwest of Valentia Island, the Skelligs are two massive rocks like mountain tops soaring up out of the Atlantic Ocean. The smaller Skellig is a bird sanctuary. It is home to many thousands of sea birds including the exotic-looking little puffins. Guillemot, razorbill, storm petrel, kittiwake, gannet and shearwater are plentiful, too. The shearwater makes a strange haunting sound at night. All of the birds spend summer on the Skelligs. Many of them spend their winters in such varied places as the west coast of Africa, South America and the Mediterranean.

The larger of the rocks, Skellig Michael, is also home to some birds, but it is as a monastic settlement that it is most famous. It is forty-four acres in area and stands 714 feet above sea level. The monastic settlement, founded by St. Fionan in the sixth century, consists of six beehive huts, two oratories and stone terraces and steps all built by the monks. There are 670 steps to be climbed in order to reach the buildings and a total of twenty-three hundred steps all over the island. One of the oratories, on a slightly lower level than most of the buildings, is called the Church of St. Michael. It was built in the eleventh century with stones taken over from the mainland, although there was no shortage of rocks on the island.

It is quite difficult to land on Skellig Michael. Even when the sea is relatively calm it takes skilled seamanship to accomplish the task. Once on the island, the atmosphere of asceticism and mystery is almost palpable. Climb the 670 well-worn steps, ascending skywards like Jacob's Ladder, and realize with every step just how austere the lives of these holy men must have been. Looking down from the seven-hundred-foot aerie, it's awesome to think that almost nothing has changed in twelve hundred years. This is the same sight St. Fionan would have seen in the sixth century.

The Vikings raided, plundered and massacred here three times; in A.D. 812, 823 and 833.

The monks stayed on Skellig Michael until the twelfth century when they moved to Ballinskellig on the mainland.

The Skelligs had an earlier history than the monastic settlement of the sixth century. Back in 1200 B.C., the Milesians, headed by Queen Scota and her nine sons, supposedly landed here on their second attempt. A number of their ships were wrecked and many of their people lost. Ir, one of the nine sons of Mil, was drowned and his body was placed on Skelligs of the Spectors as it was called. There is a belief in Irish folklore that on moonlit nights, the souls of the dead can be seen over the Skelligs on their way to Tir na nOg, in salutation to Ir.

Amergin, another of the sons of Mil, was poet, philosopher and lawgiver. He uttered an obscure poem when he first set foot on Ireland. It gives the coming of the Milesians more impor-

tance than a mere historical invasion. As translated by R. A. S.
Macalister, Amergin proclaimed:

> I am wind on the sea,
> I am ocean wave,
> I am roar of sea,
> I am bull of seven fights,
> I am vulture on cliff,
> I am dewdrop,
> I am fairest of flowers,
> I am boar for boldness,
> I am salmon in pool,
> I am lake on plain . . .
> I am a word of skill,
> I am the point of a weapon (that poureth forth
>   combat),
> I am God who fashioneth fire for a head.
> Who smoothest the ruggedness of a mountain?
> Who is He who announceth the ages of the moon?
> And who, the place where falleth the sunset?
> Who calleth the cattle from the House of Tethra?
> On whom do the cattle of Tethra smile?
> Who is the troop, who the God who fashioneth
>   edges . . . ?
> Enchantments about a spear? Enchantments of
>   wind?

I was deeply and profoundly impressed by my visit to Skelligs Michael. It is an extremely special and very moving place that touches the soul.

Memories

Travelling on his boat out to the Skelligs, I remarked to Des Lavelle that the monks who went out to live on those barren rocks eight miles off the Kerry coast were either very brave or mad. Wise man that he is, he told me to mention that again after I had climbed to the top.

The higher I climbed up the 670 steps to the top, the more the atmosphere kept changing. By the time I was walking around examining the beehive huts and the oratories I was completely awestruck.

During a light shower of rain I went into one of the beehive huts and sat down on the floor staring out the door and I got the overpowering feeling that I was not alone in there. I could sense something remarkable and very spiritual all around me and all over me, filling me with amazement and a great lightness of spirit. After the rain I emerged from the stone hut and spent the rest of my time up there and also descending again in what I remember as a spiritual glow.

On the boat back to the mainland Des Lavelle looked at me and smiled. "God is always very close up there" he said quietly.

Now I know why the monks lived on that rock.

Kenmare

Kenmare, in County Kerry, could be called the southern terminus of the Ring of Kerry. It is a very convenient base for exploring both the Iveragh Peninsula, on which the Ring of Kerry is situated and the Beara Peninsula in County Cork. The town was founded in 1670 by Sir William Petty on land assigned to him by the English government. The English settlers were ousted in 1688 by the native Irish.

A two-span concrete suspension bridge carries the main road

across the sound on the Kenmare River and through the town.

An interesting old bridge spans the Finnihy River near the site of an abbey called The Shrubberies. Here at The Shrubberies we'll find the fifty-foot stone Druid's Circle. The fifteen standing stones of the circle surround a large dolmen.

Kenmare in the shadow of the lofty Kerry mountains is beautifully situated where the Roughty River flows into the estuary of the Kenmare River. It is noted for its excellent lace making.

11

AND THUS GROWS FONDER, SWEET CORK, OF THEE

Castletownbere, County Cork

On the north shore of Bantry Bay, Castletownbere was a stronghold of the great chieftain O'Sullivan Bere.

At the Battle of Kinsale in 1601, the Irish under the renowned Ulster chieftain O'Neill, were defeated. This defeat is regarded as the end of Gaelic Ireland. After the battle, the O'Sullivan stronghold at Dunboy Castle, about two miles from Castletownbere, was attacked. The O'Sullivans withstood the siege until 18 June 1602. On that date, four thousand English troops, under the command of Sir George Carew, shattered the walls and executed the entire Irish garrison.

A little to the northwest, at Eyeries Point there is a seventeen-foot-tall Ogham stone.

Glengarriff, County Cork

The name Glengarriff means "The Rough Glen." There are boulders and rocks scattered all over the glen. This is countered by great bursts of greenery. Tall pine trees, stately oaks and elms, lovely arbutus which sheds its bark, and glistening holly abound. There is a profusion of flowers and tropical plants. Fuchsia flourishes everywhere. Being so well sheltered, Glengarriff is blessed with a very mild climate and is one of the loveliest spots in Ireland.

Not far away, out in Bantry Bay stands Garinish Island. It now belongs to the nation, but previous owners Mr. and Mrs. John Annan Bryce, helped by Harold Peto, transformed this rocky island into a tropical garden paradise. They made a beautiful Italian garden with a lily pool, a miniature Japanese garden and an overhanging rock garden. There are all kinds of exotic trees and tropical plants. Some plants come from the Antipodes and others from Antarctica. There is even a simulated Greek Temple and a Martello Tower.

George Bernard Shaw was a visitor here and wrote part of his play *Saint Joan* while visiting. Agatha Christie, when she visited the island later attributed the visit to her literary detective Hercule Poirot.

Before leaving Glengarriff take a night-time swim in the phosphorescent waters. Apparently it's an unforgettable experience.

Kinsale

The elegant town of Kinsale, on the banks of the Bandon River, is an important boating and sea-fishing centre. Built on Compass Hill, the streets of Kinsale have many eighteenth-century houses that lend elegance to the town's character. It was a seat of the Desmonds, who built Desmond Castle in the fifteenth century. Desmond Castle is also known as the French Prison because of the French prisoners who were incarcerated there during the Napoleonic Wars.

In the Battle of Kinsale in 1601, Lord Mountjoy, with twelve thousand English troops, defeated the Irish forces of Hugh O'Neill and Red Hugh O'Donnell. This defeat marked the end of the noble Gaelic Ireland and its aristocracy. The chieftains O'Neill and O'Donnell left Ireland for mainland Europe in what was to become known in Irish history as the Flight of the Earls.

In 1689, King James II landed here in Kinsale on his way to the Battle of the Boyne. He fought at Oldbridge, near Drogheda in County Louth in July 1690. After his defeat there by William of Orange, James II made his way back to Kinsale and fled from here to France in 1691.

Charles Fort, in nearby Summercove, was built by the Duke of Ormonde between 1670 and 1677. There remains the ruins of a barracks, which was occupied up until the Anglo-Irish Treaty, which was signed on 6 December 1921. A romantic "White Lady" ghost story is also associated with Charles Fort.

On 7 May 1915, a German U-boat sank the Cunard liner *Lusitania,* off Kinsale's Old Head about nine miles from the town.

Kinsale is a charming town, with good restaurants and an always festive air.

Blarney Castle built in the fifteenth century, houses the celebrated Blarney Stone. (photo provided by the Irish Tourist Board)

Blarney

Blarney was famous in days gone by for its wools and tweeds. Happily, in recent times that fame has been renewed. It is even more famous for being the home, at Blarney Castle, of the celebrated Blarney Stone. Supposedly, it bestows the gift of the gab on anyone who kisses it.

Back in the seventeenth century, one Cormac MacCarthy, who was Lord Muskerry and was known colloquially as "Blarney," lived at Blarney Castle. Cormac was possessed of great eloquence and used it very well to avoid accepting the authority of Queen Elizabeth I of England. The queen was not amused by the frequency and diversity of his verbal trickery. She was reported as saying in a fit of pique: "This is all Blarney; what he says he never means." So the gift of the gab became known as blarney.

The castle itself was built in the fifteenth century and was regarded as the strongest in Munster. It was bought in 1703 by the Jeffreys family and their descendants are the present owners.

Cork

St. Finbarr, who died in A.D. 630, founded a monastery on an island here surrounded by swampland. Perhaps that's where the city of Cork got its name. *Corcaigh* in Irish means marsh.

The monastery thrived and grew and the town sprang up around it. It became so prosperous that it came to the notice of the marauding Vikings, who plundered the monastery and the town many times. Eventually, as they began to calm down somewhat, they realized that trading was much easier on them than plundering and just as profitable. The growing town, using its harbour and all of its other attributes, became a centre of commerce. It remains a flourishing business centre to the present day.

St. Finbarr's Church of Ireland Cathedral is a nineteenth-century French Gothic structure with three spires. It was probably built on the site of the original monastery. Part of a round tower existed on the site until the foundations of the cathedral were laid.

Christ Church in South Main Street is a Norse foundation of A.D. 1050. The Red Abbey Tower on the south side of the city is part of an Augustinian abbey built around A.D. 1300.

Also in the southern area of the city, Elizabeth Fort is where the citizens of Cork gathered to defy the troops of King James I in 1605.

University College Cork, which was founded in 1845, is part of the National University of Ireland. Its lovely campus with Tudor buildings was built on the site of seventh-century Grill Abbey. The college houses a very important collection of Ogham stones. These are standing stones carved in what is generally regarded as the ancient Ogham alphabet. A very interesting portion of pavement at the college depicts the canticle of "The Three Children in the Fiery Furnace."

The main business district of Cork is situated between the north and south branches of the River Lee with numerous bridges spanning the river. Where Patrick Street and Grand Parade are located, there was a channel used by shipping up until the late eighteenth century.

Cork has a shipyard, a steelworks and chemical works but the Ford and Dunlop factories both fell victim to the recession of the 1980s. Murphy's Brewery, which makes Murphy's Stout, often referred to as Corkmen's milk, is situated at Lady's Well. It is on the site of a hospital whose well was supposed to have curative powers. No wonder it's beloved by the people of Cork, and recently, many foreign parts like Boston and New York as well.

Cork has its fair share of famous people like George James

Allman, the nineteenth-century zoologist and botanist; James Barry, the eighteenth–nineteenth-century historical painter; Dr. Hincks, the eighteenth–nineteenth-century Egyptologist. Sir Walter Scott was given the Freedom of the City in 1825. Edmund Spencer reputedly married Elizabeth Boyle here in 1594. Of course, Christy Ring, the illustrious hurler is as much a part of Cork as Murphy's Stout.

Arguably, the most famous clergyman in Cork's history is Fr. Theobald Matthew. In the nineteenth century, Fr. Matthew was second only to Dan O'Connell in national prominence. He espoused the unpopular cause of temperance and with great energy and zealousness turned the cause into a crusade. He is commemorated by a statue near Patrick's Bridge and immortalized in the song "The Boys of Fair Hill":

> The smell 'round Patrick's Bridge is wicked,
> How do Father Matthew stick it?

> —ANONYMOUS

In the Shandon district, on the north side, St. Ann's Church of Ireland, built in 1722, houses the celebrated Shandon Bells. Two sides of the tower are faced with red sandstone and the other two sides with gleaming limestone. The eight bells were made in Gloucester in England. The sixth bell bears the inscription "We were all cast at Gloucester in England. Abel Rudhall 1750." Visitors are allowed to play tunes on the bells. With its clock tower and pepper-box steeple, St. Ann's is called "The Lion of Cork." Fr. S. Mahony who died in Rome in 1866, wrote a lot of verse under the pen name Father Prout. He showed his love for Cork, whether he had his tongue in cheek or not, when he wrote "The Bells of Shandon":

> With deep affection and recollection
> I often think on those Shandon Bells

Whose sound so wild would, in days of childhood,
Ring 'round my cradle their magic spell.
On this I ponder where'er I wander,
And thus grow fonder, sweet Cork of thee,
And the Bells of Shandon that sound so grand on
The pleasant waters of the river Lee.

Corkonians, no matter to what corner of the world they may travel, never lose their deep-rooted love for, and pride in their city and the lovely River Lee on which it is built.

The fair city of Cork sits proudly on the banks of the River Lee.
(photo provided by the Irish Tourist Board)

The Banks of My Own Lovely Lee

How oft do my thoughts in their fancy take flight
To the home of my childhood away,
To the day when each patriot's vision seemed bright,

Ere I dreamed that those joys would decay.
When my heart was as light as the wild wind that
    blows
Down the Mardyke, through each elm tree,
Where we sported and played neath the green leafy
    shade
On the banks of my own lovely Lee.
Where we sported and played neath the green leafy
    shade
On the banks of my own lovely Lee.

And then in the springtime of laughter and song,
Will I ever forget the sweet hours
With the friends of my youth as we rambled along
'Mongst the green mossy banks and wild flowers.
Then too, when the evening sun sinking to rest
Sheds its golden light over the sea,
The maid with her lover the wild daisies pressed
On the banks of my own lovely Lee.
The maid with her lover the wild daisies pressed
On the banks of my own lovely Lee.

—ANONYMOUS

MEMORIES

I was taking a walk along busy Patrick Street in Cork when I heard it. Sweetening the air came a melodious, plaintive, throbbing slow air played soulfully on a fiddle. I stood transfixed for a minute or so as the melody hurried me down the years to my boyhood and a Fair Day in Keady, County Armagh, my home-town.

Amid all the noise, laughter and shouting, three musicians, a fiddler, a tin whistle player and an uilleann piper mesmerised a crowd of farmers, townspeople, cattle and horse dealers with this very same tune. I had not heard it since then, but remembered it very vividly because, like Homer's sirens, it lured me from going back to school after my lunch at home and gave me a memorable afternoon of wonderful music. Shaking myself out of my trance I set off as quickly as I could to find the source of that long-remembered melody. In an unused doorway of a shop a man in a much travelled coat was coaxing magic out of his fiddle. With his eyes closed, the music was coming from the very depths of his soul. As I joined the group of people around him, he turned in my direction, opened his eyes and smiled at me, very enigmatically, I thought. I was astounded to discover that it was the very same fiddler from that long ago Fair Day in Keady. And, I do believe he was wearing the very same coat. Neither the fiddler nor the coat had aged by a single day in all those years! I had taken on much time and wear but he had remained exactly the same.

On bending down to put some money in his cap on the ground, I discovered it had gone mysteriously, as had the fiddler.

The music lingered in the air deep into the night, but search as I would through the city of Cork, I couldn't find sight or light of the ageless fiddler.

Magic happens in Cork—very frequently.

Youghal, County Cork

Youghal is the Anglicized version of *Eochaill,* which means "Yew Wood." The town stands on the west side of the River Blackwater where it flows into Youghal Harbour. It had a bustling civic life before the fourteenth century and is liberally dotted with antiquities.

Situated about two miles northwest of the town, Rincrew Abbey was founded in the twelfth century by Raymond Fitzgerald who was known as Raymond le Gros.

Youghal has the largest medieval parish church in Ireland. The Collegiate Church of St. Mary was built in the thirteenth century. It was restored in the fifteenth century and again in the nineteenth. There is a large separate belfry tower with walls eight feet thick. Among the numerous other features, there is a monument to the memory of Catherine, Countess of Desmond, who died after a fall from a cherry tree at the age of 147!

At the north end of Main Street are the ruins of North Abbey, a Dominican monastery that was founded in 1268.

Main Street is spanned by a wide arch which supports a four-story building called "The Clock Gate," which was built in 1771. Nearby is the fifteenth-century Tynte's Castle. The town walls also date from the fifteenth century.

In 1579 the town was sacked by the Earl of Desmond, who had joined the southern Geraldines in their rebellion. All of the inhabitants fled save for one old friar. The English retook the sacked town, invited the inhabitants to return and left three hundred troops to protect them. Having confiscated the Desmond estate, the Crown bestowed forty-two thousand acres on Sir Walter Raleigh for his part in opposing the Desmonds. Raleigh, who planted the first potatoes in Ireland, later sold his estate to the earl of Cork. Myrtle Grove, Raleigh's home, where he entertained Spenser, is not open to the public.

Oliver Cromwell, during his barbarous campaign in Ireland in the mid-seventeenth century, used Youghal as a headquarters. He departed from Youghal on his return to England in 1650, leaving his son-in-law Ireton in charge.

The Presentation Sisters have made Youghal Lace famous for over a hundred years. In recent times, Youghal has developed a very fine carpet industry that is known world wide.

12

There's None to Compare with the Waterford Boys

Lismore, County Waterford

Lismore is nestled on the banks of Munster's River Blackwater. St. Carthac built a monastery here in the seventh century. In the ensuing years as many as twenty churches flourished here. By the twelfth century, Lismore had established its reputation as a centre for education and religion.

King Henry II invaded Ireland in 1171. He was joined by, among others, Raymond le Gros (Raymond Fitzgerald) and his troops. Henry remained in Ireland for only seven months before he returned to England. His followers continued the conquest of Ireland. In 1173, Raymond le Gros arrived in the lovely town of Lismore and plundered it.

Lismore Castle was built in 1185 by King John. He chose a very dramatic site for it on a sheer cliff overhanging the Blackwater. The castle and estate eventually came into the possession of Sir Walter Raleigh. It was probably given to him and he in turn sold all to the earl of Cork in 1602.

Robert Boyle the noted chemist was born here in 1627. He was the author of Boyle's Law which stated: "When gas is at a constant temperature the product of the pressure and volume of a given mass remains constant." Boyle, who was a devout

Christian paid for the translation of the Bible into Gaelic and also its publication.

The famous fifteenth-century *Book of Lismore* and the Lismore Crozier were found in the castle walls in 1814.

Ardmore, County Waterford

St. Declan, who was one of the very few pre-Patrician Christians in Ireland, founded a monastery in Ardmore in the fifth century. Parts of the remains of that monastery include St. Declan's Oratory and the Little Peaked Building which is a small early church.

Ardmore is noted for the ninety-six-foot-high round tower, which is one of the most complete in Ireland. One of the interesting features of the tower is that it has four separate stories. Some of the projecting stones on the inside are carved with grotesque figures.

An early thirteenth-century cathedral has Romanesque sculptures set in the west wall in two tiers. They include *The Judgement of Solomon, The Adoration of the Magi* and *The Archangel Michael Weighing Souls* on the top tier. On the lower tier, Adam and Eve are distinguishable. The church also has two Ogham stones.

In 1642 the church and the round tower were used as shelter for the Catholic army who were fighting against the forces of King Charles I. The Catholic forces surrendered to the English with one of the provisions of the surrender being mercy for those inside. Nevertheless, 140 men were put to the sword by the English troops.

Dungarvan, County Waterford

The town of Dungarvan is situated in an area called The Decies. The area was named after a tribe from Meath who settled here in the third century.

King John's Castle was built as a stronghold in the late 1180s. The castle suffered during the Cromwellian era in the mid-seventeenth century. It was spared from serious destruction because Cromwell himself saw a woman drink his health at the town gate. Remnants of the town walls still remain, part of it being called "Dead Walk." I suppose there is a story connected with the name, but unfortunately, I don't know it.

In 1290 John Fitzthomas Fitzgerald built an Augustinian priory. A tower from that priory is incorporated into a modern church.

There is a single-arched bridge with a seventy-five-foot span that was built in 1815 at a cost of fifty thousand pounds.

Take the eight-mile drive from Dungarvan out to the impressive Helvick Head and be rewarded with beautiful views of Dungarvan Bay. On the way is the village of Ring which is the heart of the Gaeltacht (Irish speaking area). It has a well known and highly regarded Gaelic college. Traditional music is not only alive but quite vibrant in Ring—a great place to while away long, drowsy and very pleasant evenings and indeed many wonderful nights as well.

Built in 1003 by Reginald the Norseman, Reginald's Tower stands eighty feet high in the city of Waterford. (photo provided by the Irish Tourist Board)

Waterford

Waterford was founded by the Vikings in about A.D. 914. The Rivers Barrow, Nore and Suir flow into its harbour. The Vikings found all three convenient for plundering the surrounding countryside. Centuries later Waterford was conquered by the Anglo-Normans. In the eighteenth century, Waterford had a glass industry considered to be the finest in Europe. It was destroyed in the early nineteenth century by the imposition of heavy taxes. Then in 1947 the glass and crystal industry was restored and its fame spread around the world. Today, the name Waterford is synonymous with the apex of the glass and crystal industry.

Reginald's Tower was built in 1003 by Reginald the Norseman. It is, of course, circular, stands about eighty feet high and is the best-known landmark in Waterford. In 1955, Reginald's Tower was converted into a civic museum to commemorate Waterford's 750th anniversary as a chartered city.

King Henry II landed at Waterford in 1171 with five hundred knights and four thousand troops for his invasion of Ireland. The justification for the invasion was not made public until during a famous synod that was convened in Waterford in 1175. A papal bull from Pope Adrian IV, an English pope named Nicholas Breakspeare, was read. In the bull which was dated 1155, the pope requested Henry to reclaim Ireland for Rome. The Irish church was supposedly in revolt. The existence of that papal bull has been very seriously doubted. Some have thought that it may have been forged. No copy of it can be found in the archives in Rome, according to the book *Ireland Past and Present*, by Conyngham, Curtin, Parnell and Redpath, published in New York in 1887. It is strange, and rather convenient that a papal bull dated 1155 was not made public until 1175, twenty years later.

Waterford has a very successful Light Opera Festival every September.

The Waterford Boys

Now boys for diversion we're all met together,
I'll tell you from Waterford's whether I came.
I crossed the big ocean in dark gloomy weather,
My heart it was light and my pockets the same.
Sad leaving old Ireland, once more on dry land,
By the roadside a tavern I happened to spy,
And as I was melting, my pockets I felt in
For the price of a drink I was mortually* dry.

Chorus:
For we are the boys for fun with an element,

*This colloquialism for *mortally* is generally used in this song.

Drinking and dancing and all other joys.
For ructions, destructions, diversions and devil-
ment,
There's none to compare with the Waterford boys.

In the tavern I rolled, out the master he strolled,
"Good morning to you sir," says I "if you please,
Provide me a bed and give me some bread,
With a bottle of porter and a small lump of cheese.
Now times they are queer, provisions are dear,
If I get the bread without cheese, I'm content."
Says the landlord "You're right" and he fetched me
the bite
And I rolled up my sleeves and at it I went.

Chorus:

My bread and cheese ended, I then condescended
To seek for repose, I called for a light,
And soon in a doze from under the clothes,
I popped on my toes and I soon had a light.
Now waking from sleeping, I heard something
creeping,
Meandering and wandering around the bedpost,
With a tearing and scratching, says I "I'm a watch-
ing,
By my conscience you've very long claws for a
ghost."

Chorus:

My breath I suspended, the noise it soon ended,
I ventured to peep from beneath the bedclothes,
*Meelia** murder, what's that? And a jumping jack rat

*The meaning of this word is unknown; probably a corruption of an Irish word.

With a bounce from the floor, lit on top of my nose.
"Thunder take you" says I "for a grey longtailed
　vagabond,
Take that and that" as I jumped on the floor,
Shouting "Murder and fire, Jim, Jerry, Mariah,
Your rats they are eating me up, by the score."

Chorus:

Now the landlord polite, he came up with a light,
Says I "I'm being eaten and must be away."
Says he "Before going, I'll have you to know
For supper and bed you've five shillings to pay."
"Five shillings for what?" says I "Now be aisy,
And don't be disgracing yourself, if you please,
When I can't sleep for rats, you've a brazen old face
To charge me five shillings for plain bread and
　cheese."

Chorus:

"Oh perish these rats, I wish they would leave me,
They've ruined my trade, till I'm not worth a rap."
Says I "The five shillings if you will forgive me
I'll give you a plan to keep out every rat."
He agreed. "Then" says I, "to supper invite them,
Plain bread and cheese set before them be sure,
Don't mind if they're willing, just charge them five
　shillings
And devil the rat will you ever see more."

Chorus:

—ANONYMOUS

Memories

It was towards the end of August and I was driving south from Armagh down the east coast. The day was very pleasant, the countryside looked lovely, the music on the car radio was relatively good, and I was really enjoying the drive.

After stopping to eat somewhere in County Waterford I started off happily once more. A mile or two down the road I gradually became aware of a very steady, quiet, metallic knocking sound which got a little louder when I went around a bend in the road. A little flutter of apprehension started to tickle me in the solar plexus, so I pulled into the side of the road and stopped the car. Fearing that the engine oil might be low, which would cause the bearings to rattle, I got out and checked. To my surprise the amount of oil in the engine was fine. There seemed to be nothing loose around the engine that would cause the rattle and after a perfunctory look, nothing loose underneath the car either.

I got back into the car and started off cautiously and for a few minutes everything was quiet, the knocking sound seemed to have stopped. Ten minutes later the knocking started again and the butterflies resumed fluttering in my stomach. Realizing there was nothing I could do myself, I decided to drive on to where I could get some help. I was becoming gradually more tense waiting for the engine to sieze up, blow up or fall out of the car, leaving me on a country road somewhere in County Waterford and dusk beginning to fall.

I eventually made it to Waterford city and a garage where, luckily, there was a mechanic working late. Approaching him as he was bent over a car engine with a work light, he heard me and on turning around and seeing me his face broke into a brilliant smile. "Just the very bloody man" says he "give us a bar of a song while you're standing there doing nothing." I explained that I wasn't in much form for singing at the moment as I seemed to have developed serious car trouble. After explaining about the metallic knocking and about the oil being okay, he said he'd better hear it for himself. Bursting into a loud rollicking song he screeched away in a cloud of dust, driving my poor ailing car.

He was back in five minutes with a great smile on his face. "I have good news and bad news" he said. "The good news is that your metallic knocking was caused by an empty Coca-Cola bottle under the driver's seat that was rattling against the metal. The bad news is that you'll be travelling on and me hoping we might have a great singing session here in Waterford tonight." He wouldn't take any money for his trouble so I thanked him very sincerely for curing my car trouble and added that maybe his bad news could be cured as well.

It was . . . we had a mighty night's singing!

13

THE GOLDEN VALE

Clonmel

Clonmel is a very handsome town in the southern end of County Tipperary. The name Clonmel comes from the Irish *Cluain Meala,* which means "Pasture of Honey." No doubt, the town got its name from where it is situated in the rich green valley of the River Suir (pronounced sure). There was a lot of yellow sandstone used in many of the buildings of the town and this imbues its well laid out streets with a lovely warmth.

Parts of the fourteenth-century walls are still standing, including the West Gate, which was rebuilt in 1831. The walls were last used in a defensive capacity in 1798. Cromwell attacked and took the town in 1650, but suffered the loss of two thousand men.

In the early years of the nineteenth century, an Italian immigrant named Charles Bianconi arrived in Clonmel. He was a picture framer by trade. In 1815, he set up a horse-drawn transportation system with headquarters in Hearn's Hotel in Parnell Street. Fares worked out at about two pence a mile and soon the service covered most of the province of Munster. The Bianconi Coach Service prospered until the advent of the railway. Mr. Bianconi became a rich man and was elected Mayor of Clonmel.

The town has had its share of literary connections. Laurence Sterne, the author of *Tristram Shandy* was born here in

1713. Anthony Trollope, the prolific nineteenth-century writer, whose works like *Barchester Towers, Phineas Finn* and *An Old Man's Love,* made him famous, lived here. George Borrow, who wrote *Wild Wales* and *Lavengro,* attended grammar school in Clonmel around 1815. He learned the Irish language and it was a passion of his until he died.

Slievenaman (The Mountain of the Women) stands about seven miles northeast of the town. The mountain supposedly got its name when Finn MacCool (MacCumhal), the leader of the Fianna warriors had the women of Ireland race up the mountain with his offer to marry the winner. The eventual winner is reputed to have been Grainne, the daughter of the Irish King Cormac.

Grubb's Cave, near Clogheen to the southwest of Clonmel, is the burial place of one Samuel Grubb, who owned the local Castle Grace. Grubb requested that he be buried standing upright so that he could, as he put it, "overlook my land." Well I suppose it's the next best thing if you can't take it with you.

The Convict of Clonmel

How hard is my fortune, and vain my repining!
The strong rope of death for this young neck is
    twining.
My strength all departed, my cheeks sunk and sal-
    low,
While I languish in chains in the jail of Cluain Meala.

No boy in the village was ever yet milder;
I'd play with a child and my sport be no wilder;
I'd dance without tiring from morning to even,
And my goal ball I'd strike to the lightning of
    heaven.

At my bedfoot decaying my hurley is lying;
Through the boys of the village my goal ball is fly-
    ing.

My horse 'mong the neighbours neglected may
   fallow,
While I pine here in chains in the jail of Cluain Meala.

Next Sunday the Patron at home will be keeping,
The young active hurlers the field will be sweeping;
With the dance of fair maidens, the evening they'll
   hallow,
While this heart once so gay will be cold in Cluain
   Meala.

—J. J. CALLINAN

Rising majestically out of the Plain of Tipperary, the Rock of Cashel is considered one of Ireland's most historical sites. (photo provided by the Irish Tourist Board)

Cashel

The magnificent Rock of Cashel is considered one of Ireland's most historical sites. It rises majestically some two hundred feet out of the Plain of Tipperary and dominates the entire area. The sight of the Rock arrests attention from any road leading to the town. Cashel was the home of the Kings of Munster from A.D. 370 to 1101, when King Murtagh O'Brien granted the Rock to the church. Many of the early kings were also bishops.

The buildings that crown the Rock include: A round tower built in the tenth century; the Hall of Vicar's Choral, which has been beautifully restored; and the elegant Cormac's Chapel with very interesting carved stone doorways and ceiling. It was built in 1127 by King and Bishop Cormac MacCarthy, and consecrated for use in 1134. Part of the east wall of the chapel was rebuilt in 1875. Also on the Rock there is St. Patrick's Cross, which is of eleventh-century origin and a twelfth-century high cross, which stands near the cathedral. In the early fifteenth century, Archbishop O'Hedigan built what is called the Archbishop's Palace. He included a number of hidden passages in the walls of the building which indicates just how uncertain the times were.

The Rock of Cashel, as can be imagined, was the scene of many significant events. In the fifth century, St. Patrick came here to preach; the glorious Brian Boru was crowned king of Munster in the early eleventh century; English King Henry II came here in the twelfth century, raiding. Gerald, the Earl of Kildare came here in 1495 and burned the cathedral. He told King Henry VII that he burned it because he thought the archbishop was inside. Murrough O'Brien, the Earl of Inchiquin, plundered and burned here in 1647, damaging many of the buildings. Afterwards the cathedral was only used intermittently. It was finally abandoned in 1749.

In the early seventeenth century, Myler McGrath, who became known as "The Scoundrel of Cashel," was Catholic bishop here. Because he thought he could make more money, he renounced Catholicism and became Protestant Bishop of Cashel. Being a man of many accomplishments, he managed to hold a Catholic bishopric in the northern part of the country at the same time. He seldom, if ever, visited his Catholic diocese. The revenues from both of his flocks, and the lands he controlled, enabled him to continue to live the good life in Cashel.

Contemplating where he should be buried, he chose a tomb that already held the remains of one of his predecessors. This posed no problem for Myler. He had the remains removed and he is buried in that notable tomb.

In the chaos he caused and communications being what they were at that time, it took seven years for Rome to find out about his double dealings. Rome immediately excommunicated him. He was not concerned by the excommunication and continued to live happily in Cashel until he died in 1622. Before his death, he recanted and once again became a Catholic.

The town of Cashel, which is completely dominated by the magnificence and importance of the Rock, has a number of historical buildings of note. Quirke's Castle, which is now an hotel, is a fifteenth-century tower standing in Main Street. Just at the foot of the Rock, Cashel Palace, the former home of the Protestant archbishops of Cashel, is now also an hotel. It was built in 1730 and is beautifully furnished in the style of the eighteenth century. The thirteenth-century Dominican friary was founded by Archbishop David MacKelly and is situated just off the main street.

In the meadows just below the Rock is Hore Abbey, a Cistercian monastery also of the thirteenth century.

Down below the Rock, on the opposite side to Hore Abbey, Comhaltas Ceoltori Eireann, Society of Irish Musicians, has built a beautiful new complex called Bru Boru. It has a theatre, shop, meeting hall and restaurant. Here they carry on their great work of preserving, teaching and reinvigorating Irish traditional music, song and dance. Long may they prosper in keeping a vital part of the cultural heritage alive. The nation owes them a deep debt of gratitude.

Kilkenny

Kilkenny is known as "The Marble City" because of the black marble quarries about half a mile from the city. The little winding lanes, known locally as "slips," give Kilkenny a sort of medieval air. Its elegant Georgian houses make it one of the most charming cities in Ireland.

Back in 1391, the Earl of Ormonde bought the town. His descendants added to it and made it a very important place. In the early years of the fourteenth century, King Edward III of England had divided the part of Ireland that he controlled into three earldoms: Kildare, Desmond and Ormonde. Kilkenny naturally became the centre and chief town of Ormonde. In 1329, James Butler, the Earl of Ormonde, became Lord Lieutenant of Ireland. Gradually the town became a chief seat of government, even rivaling Dublin. Regular meetings of the Irish Parliament took place here.

In the year 1366, Lionel, the duke of Clarence, earl of Ulster, lord of Connacht and lord lieutenant of Ireland, summoned a famous meeting in Kilkenny. They passed what has become known as the infamous Statute of Kilkenny. This forbade any English settler to adopt an Irish name, wear Irish apparel or use the Irish language. All men (and I suppose women) of Irish blood were forbidden to live in walled towns. If a settler married an Irish woman it was considered high treason.

The city was besieged and captured by Oliver Cromwell's army in 1650.

Standing in a commanding position on the banks of the

River Nore, Kilkenny Castle was the home of the Butler family since the fourteenth century. It was built between 1192 and 1207 by William, Earl Marshall, who was Strongbow's son-in-law. There is an art gallery housed in the castle now. The windows of the castle look down on Kilkenny College where Dean Jonathan Swift and Congreve were both educated. The castle was completely remodelled during the nineteenth century. All that remains of the old building are three towers and part of the curtain wall. It's still a very imposing building standing in fifteen acres of parkland.

During the seventeenth century war, between the English king and Parliament, Kilkenny was the seat of the Confederate Parliament. This was the last native Irish parliament with representatives from all of the countries and important towns in Ireland.

Kilkenny has three divisions: Irishtown to the north has St. Canice's Cathedral; High Town is to the south of Irishtown and separated from it by the Bregagh River; the third division is east of the River Nore and contains the Priory of St. John.

In the sixth century, St. Canice, the patron saint of Kilkenny, founded a monastery and the present St. Canice's Cathedral was built on the same site in the thirteenth century. There remains a hundred-foot-high round tower believed to be from the original building. St. Canice's Library houses some three thousand books from the sixteenth and seventeenth centuries.

The Franciscan Grey Friary, now called St. Francis's was built on a point of land between the Rivers Nore and Bregagh in 1231. It is now in the possession of a brewery.

The Dominican Black Friary was built in 1225 by the Earl of Pembroke. Black Freren Gate still stands as part of the old town walls. In 1540, the year after the dissolution of the monasteries, Henry VIII granted the site of the Blackfriars Monastery to Kilkenny Corporation.

The Priory of St. John was built in the thirteenth century and stands east of the River Nore.

There were a number of almshouses in Kilkenny. They were

called "switzers." The Shee Almshouse, probably funded by the prominent Shee family, was built in 1582 and has St. Mary's steps leading to the back of it.

A number of famous old inns sprang up in Kilkenny during the sixteenth and seventeenth centuries. Archer's Inn in High Street and Rothe's Inn in Parliament Street were both built in 1594. The most famous, Kyteler's Inn in St. Kieran Street, was built in 1639.

Kyteler's Inn was supposedly named for Dame Alice Kyteler. In the early fourteenth century she allegedly poisoned four husbands and was convicted of sorcerey. Dame Alice escaped but her maid, named Petronella, was burned at the stake in High Street.

James Hoban, the architect of the White House in Washington, D.C., was born near Kilkenny.

The Boys of Kilkenny

Oh the boys of Kilkenny are neat roving blades,
And whenever they meet with the dear little maids,
They kiss them and coax them and spend their
    money free;
Oh! Of all towns in Ireland, Kilkenny for me.

Through the town of Kilkenny there runs a clear
    stream,
In the town of Kilkenny there lives a fair dame,
Her cheeks are like roses, her lips much the same,
Or a dish of fresh strawberries smothered in
    cream.

Her eyes are as black as Kilkenny's famed coal,
And they, through my poor heart have burnt a big
    hole;
Her mind, like the river, is deep, clear and pure,
But her heart is as hard as its marble, I'm sure.

Oh! Kilkenny's a fine town, that shines where it
   stands,
And the more I think of it the more my heart
   warms;
If I was in Kilkenny, I'd feel right at home,
For it's there I'd get sweethearts, but here I get none.

—ANONYMOUS

MEMORIES

On the day after Christmas, known as Boxing Day and also St. Stephen's
Day, I was passing through a town in County Kilkenny and I encountered
a procession of Wren Boys for the first time. Surprised and delighted by
the singing and the colour on the street I pulled my car into the side and
got out to investigate.

   There was a crowd of twenty or thirty people, mostly young, all dressed
in motley costumes. A fiddle and a harmonica were being played to ac-
company the spirited singing. There was a young man carrying a holly
branch all decorated with multi-coloured ribbons and pieces of paper. Fas-
cinated by the happy group, I joined them as they entered a pub where
they were very warmly greeted. I approached a young couple who were
part of the group and enquired of them if they would explain what this
jollification was all about. They were not only willing to tell me about it
but were also quite knowledgeable about it.

   The group was collectively called The Wren Boys, and girls too, indeed.
Every year on Wren Day, or St. Stephen's Day as it's known to the rest of
Christendom, a ritual that has been orally passed down from pre-Christian
times, and possibly as far back as the Stone Age, is re-enacted. The ancient
people at the time of the shortest days of the year (the Winter Solstice)
hunted and caught a tiny bird, the wren. They put him in the middle of
an evergreen branch, holly or mistletoe, decorated the dead wren and the
greenery with the brightest things they could find, paraded through their
community chanting and buried their little symbol, keeping their colourful bush. The tiny bird, the wren, being so small, as was the amount of

daylight at that time of the year, was regarded as a symbol of the old Sun's divinity. The old Sun died on the shortest day of the year (21 December) and a new Sun was born to the goddess Anu (the Earth Mother) on 22 December, when their god the Sun, began to return to their world. They buried the old Sun (the wren) who had died, and triumphantly carried the symbolic new Sun, represented by the evergreen and it's light (the coloured ribbons), back to a place of honour in their community.

The present-day Wren Boys visit private houses and businesses, sing the "Wren Song" and other ditties, and ask for "a penny to bury the wren." Whatever money they may collect is given to a worthwhile charity. The whole group, including anyone who wants to participate, has a great time singing and dancing and making merry to brighten the darkest days of the year.

The Wren Boys tradition was not known where I was born and raised, but the ceremony is a wonderful occurence that could easily be started in any part of the world.

14

At the Foot of Mount Leinster

New Ross, County Wexford

New Ross got its name from the Irish *Rhos Mhic Thriuin,* which means "The wood of the son of Treon." It is situated on a steep hill on the banks of the River Barrow and is noted for its narrow winding streets. At one time, it was a very important inland port, rivaling Waterford. It was connected to Dublin via navagation of the River Barrow and the Grand Canal. More recently, it was noted for the manufacturing of sea-going barges.

In the sixth century, during the reign of King Diarmud, St. Abban founded a monastery here.

The town, itself, was founded by Strongbow's daughter, Isabella de Clare, the countess of Leinster. Strongbow, of course, was Richard de Clare, earl of Pembroke. Isabella's cenotaph was here in New Ross, where she died in 1220.

New Ross Castle was an Anglo-Norman stronghold and had a garrison of five thousand pikemen, bowmen and horsemen. The town and the castle suffered great damage during the Cromwellian invasion. During a particularly heavy bombardment by Cromwell's artillery in 1649, three cannon balls lodged in one of the gates of the mile-long Norman walls. It became known and is still known as Three Bullet Gate. Much of the town was destroyed by fire during the rebellion of the United Irishmen in 1798.

About four miles south of New Ross, is the ancestral home of President John F. Kennedy, in Dunganstown. The 480-acre John F. Kennedy Park is also here. A 310-acre arboretum and a 110-acre forest garden help to make up this beautiful memorial to the late president and his family.

Wexford

The Norsemen built this town and called it Waesfjord. The long narrow main street with its picturesque old shop fronts, lends the town a great charm.

A church built by the Vikings in 1035 is now called St. Doologue's Church. It is considered to be the smallest parish in the world with its entire jurisdiction covering all of three acres.

Portions of the Augustinian Selskar Abbey still exist. This is where the first Anglo-Irish Treaty was signed in 1169.

In the Irish national consciousness Wexford will always and ever be associated with the rebellion of The United Irishmen in 1798.

The Boys of Wexford

In comes the captain's daughter
The captain of the Yoes,
Saying "Brave United Irishmen
We'll ne'er again be foes.
A thousand pounds I'll give
If you will fly from home with me,
I'll dress myself in man's attire
And fight for liberty."

Chorus:
We are the Boys of Wexford
Who fought with heart and hand
To burst in twain the galling chain
And free our native land.

I want no gold my maiden fair,
To fly from home with thee;
Your shining eyes will be my prize,
More dear than gold to me.
I want no gold to nerve my arm,
To do a true man's part,
To free my land I'd gladly give
The red drops from my heart.

Chorus:

And when we left our cabins, boys,
We left with right good will,
To see our friends and neighbours
That were at Vinegar Hill.
A young man from our Irish ranks,
A cannon he let go;
He shot it into Lord Mountjoy,
A tyrant he laid low.

Chorus:

We bravely fought and conquered
New Ross and Wexford town;
Three Bullet Gate for years to come
Will speak for our renown;
Through Walpole's Horse and Walpole's Foot,
On Tubberneering's* day,

---

*Tubberneering is a place in Co. Wexford.

Depending on the long, bright pike,
We cut our gory way.

Chorus:

And Oulart's name shall be their shame,
Whose steel we ne'er did fear,
For every man could do his part
Like Forth and Shelmalier.
And if for want of leaders
We lost at Vinegar Hill,
We're ready for another fight
And love our country still!

Chorus:

—ROBERT DWYER JOYCE

In that rebellion, the pikemen of the United Irishmen held the town of Wexford for a month. Finally, about one hundred citizens were killed by the crown forces on the bridge and their bodies thrown into the river. In the Bullring is a statue of *The Irish Pikeman* by the artist Oliver Sheppard. It commemorates the men and women who fought so bravely in May and June of 1798.

Oscar Wilde's mother, who was known by the pen name "Speranza," was born in the Bullring. Her cousin, the nineteenth-century Arctic explorer, Sir Robert J. McClure, who discovered the Northwest Passage in 1851, was also born in Wexford. John Barry, the founder of the American Navy was Wexford born and his statue stands in The Crescent.

The Wexford Festival of Art and Music takes place annually from the last Sunday in October to the first Sunday in November.

Carlow

In the fourteenth century, the English enclaves within, roughly, a fifty-mile radius of Dublin, became known as "The Pale." It reached from parts of County Louth in the north, through parts of counties Meath, Dublin, Kildare, Wicklow and into the town of Carlow. The Pale was, strategically, a very strong base for the English forces in Ireland. Carlow, on the east bank of the River Barrow, was a frontier town of The Pale. There is still an underlying English ambience to the town of Carlow that belies a lot of its history.

Carlow Castle was built between 1207 and 1213. It was both Anglo-Norman and an English stronghold during the Middle Ages. All that remains of the castle is half of the keep.

In 1814 a Dr. Philip Middleton wished to turn the keep into a lunatic asylum. To facilitate his idea of having an open-plan ward system, he wanted to reduce the thickness of the walls. In his efforts to do so he blew up the keep!

There were many battles around Carlow between the natives and the occupying armies from the fourteenth through the seventeenth century.

The first real engagement of the United Irishmen's 1798 rebellion was fought in Tullow Street in Carlow. It spread to neighbouring Enniscorthy and Wexford town. In Graiguecullen Churchyard, a Celtic cross memorial stands in tribute to the 417 Carlow men who were killed in the uprising.

St. Patrick's Training College, which opened in 1795, was the first such facility for Catholic clergymen in the country.

During drainage of the River Barrow many stone and bronze artifacts were discovered. They are on display in the National Museum in Dublin.

About two miles east of Carlow a huge dolmen stands. A massive capstone, weighing about one hundred tons, sits on five granite uprights. It is called Browne's Hill Dolmen and is named after the Georgian mansion that stands near it. This huge monument is reputed to be the largest dolmen in Europe.

Follow Me up to Carlow

Lift MacCathair Og your face,
Brooding o'er the old disgrace
That black Fitzwilliam stormed your place
And drove you to the fern.
Grey said victory was sure,
Soon the firebrand he'd secure,
Until he met at Glenmalure
Fiach McHugh O'Byrne.

> *Chorus:*
> Curse and swear Lord Kildare,
> Fiach will do what Fiach will dare,
> Now Fitzwilliam have a care,
> Fallen is your star low.
> Up with halbred, out with sword,
> On we'll go, for by the Lord,
> Fiach McHugh has given the word
> "Follow me up to Carlow."

See the swords of Glen Imail,
Flashing o'er the English Pale,
See the children of the Gael,
Beneath O'Byrne's banners.
Rooster of a fighting stock,
Would you let an English cock
Crow out upon an Irish rock?
Fly up and teach him manners!

> *Chorus:*

From Tassagart to Clonmore
Flows a stream of Saxon gore,
Oh! great is Rory Og O'Moore
At sending loons to Hades.
Lane is sick and Lane has fled,
Now for black Fitzwilliam's head,
We'll send it over dripping red
To Liza and her ladies.

Chorus:

—P. J. McCALL

15

Sweet Vales and Glens

Arklow, Avoca, Rathdrum, Avondale and Glendalough

The town of Arklow, a very important seaside resort and boat-building centre, was founded by the Norsemen. It is also well known for its pottery.

After the Anglo-Norman invasion in the late twelfth century, one of the strongest Ormonde fortresses in the country was built here. It was taken over by the Fitzwalters, who were ancestors of the Butlers. The fortress, which withstood many attacks from native and foreigner alike, was destroyed by Cromwell's army in 1649. Its ruins stand on a rocky ledge overlooking the Avoca River.

Near the present parochial house, there are the remains of a thirteenth-century Dominican friary.

Two and a half miles northwest of the town, Shelton Abbey is now a state forestry centre. After the Battle of the Boyne in 1690, the defeated King James II is supposed to have rested at the abbey.

Running north and west from Arklow, the exquisite Vale of Avoca was made famous by a song written in 1807 by Thomas Moore. There is a bust in memory of the poet near where the

Avonmore and the Avonbeg Rivers meet to form the Avoca. An old tree stump, known as "Moore's Tree," is reputed to be where Moore was sitting when he was inspired to write his lovely "Meeting of the Waters":

> There is not in the wide world a valley so sweet,
> As that vale in whose bosom the bright waters
>   meet.

Farther up the valley the town of Rathdrum stands almost in the shadow of Lugnaquilla, at 3,040 feet, the pride of the Wicklow Mountains. On a ridge in the mountains, a fourteen-foot boulder lies for all to see. It's called "The Mottha Stone" and is supposed to be the throwing stone of the giant Finn MacCool.

Nearby is Avondale House where Charles Stewart Parnell was born in 1846. Parnell, a social reformer, was, arguably, the greatest political mind Ireland has ever produced. He was certainly the most influential. After a long, hard fought battle in the English Parliament he had come within a hair's breadth of winning complete autonomy for Ireland. He fell in love and had an affair with a married woman called Catherine O'Shea. The affair caused his political downfall and dashed the hopes, once again, of the desire of the Irish people for control over their own destiny.

A short distance northwest of Rathdrum is lovely Glendalough. Here in the sixth century, St. Kevin built a church on the Upper Lake. Later, when his following began to grow, he founded a monastery in the lower part of the glen. A fairly large dependent community grew around the monastery. Very little, if any, of the original buildings remain.

A seventh-century cathedral is the largest building in the settlement. For six hundred years this was used as a cathedral church until, in the thirteenth century, the See of Glendalough was amalgamated with the See of Dublin.

St. Kevin's Church is distinguished by its high pitched stone roof. His "Bed" is a seven-by-four-foot cave in a cliff some thirty feet above the water.

Close by St. Kevin's Church, the remains of a small church called St. Ciaran's can be found. It was burned in 1163.

St. Saviour's Church was founded by Archbishop Laurence O'Toole in the twelfth century. It was restored in 1875 by the Board of Works.

The settlement was burned and abandoned in 1398.

The 103-foot-tall round tower was recapped in the original mica slate in 1876.

St. Kevin was a hermit. He came to this beautiful spot to find peace and tranquility for his meditations and also to forgo the joys of love. As folklore has it, he was pursued by a temptress called Kathleen, who had red hair and "unholy blue" eyes. There is a song about Kathleen's pursuit of St Kevin.

St. Kevin and Kathleen

In Glendalough lived a young saint,
In the odour of sanctity dwelling,
An old-fashioned odour, which now,
We seldom or never are smelling.
He lived in a hole in the wall,
A life of ferocious austerity,
He suffered from bile and from gall,
And on women he looked with asperity.

> *Chorus:*
> Right fol-de-dol-lol-de-dol-day,
> Right fol-de-dol-lol-de-dol-addy,
> Right fol-de-dol-lol-de-dol-day
> Right fol-de-dol-lol-de-dol-addy.

There was a young woman one day,
Was walking along by the lake, sir,
She looked hard at Kevin, they say,

But St. Kevin no notice did take, sir.
When she found looking hard wouldn't do,
She looked soft, in the old sheep's eye fashion,
But with all her sheep's eyes, she could not
In St. Kevin find signs of red passion.

Chorus:

"You're a very fine fisher" says Kate,
"It's yourself that knows well how to hook 'em,
But when you have landed them neat,
Won't you want a young woman to cook 'em?"
Said the saint "I am serious inclined,
I intend taking orders for life, dear."
"Only marry" says Kate, "and you'll find
You'll get orders enough from your wife, dear."

Chorus:

"You shall never be flesh of my flesh,"
Says the saint with a thundering groan, sir;
"I see that myself" answered Kate,
"I can only be bone of your bone, sir.
And even your bones are so scarce,"
Said Kate, at her answers so glib, sir,
"That I think you would not be the worse
Of a little additional rib, sir."

Chorus:

The saint in a rage, siezed the lass,
He gave her a twirl 'round his head, sir,
And before Dr. Arnott's invention,
Prescribed her a watery bed, sir.
Oh! cruel St. Kevin, for shame!
When a lady her heart came to barter,

You should have been heard to proclaim
That you'd bow to the Order of Garter.

Chorus:

—ANONYMOUS

The Curragh, County Kildare

Lying just east of the town of Kildare is the six-mile-long Curragh. It is a green and fertile plain that is the very heart of Ireland's renowned thoroughbred horse industry. Sheep and cattle are put out to pasture here to take advantage of the luscious grazing. On the well-kept horse paths, the cream of Ireland's magnificent horses train and exercise. The Irish National Stud is nearby.

The Curragh Racecourse is the unquestioned capital of the sport of kings and hosts such important races as the Irish Derby.

The great strategic military importance of The Curragh of Kildare has been recognized for many centuries. The present army camp, which is probably the most significant centre of the Irish Military, was taken over from British forces in 1922. Many young Irish soldiers who were stationed here, have served with distinction with the United Nations peace-keeping forces all over the world.

A few miles to the northwest, the Hill of Allen, according to folklore, was the home of Finn MacCool, the leader of the third-century warriors, the Fianna.

Naas, County Kildare

The name Naas (pronounced nace) is from the Irish *An Nas,* which means the Assembly Place. In ancient times it was the meeting place for great assemblies of state.

The North Mote is the remains of a rath, or hill-fort, from the royal residence of the Fitzgeralds. It was built on the site of the ancient seat of the kings of Leinster.

St. Patrick stayed at Naas at one time. St. David's Church is supposedly built on the site where St. Patrick had set up his camp. The rectory of the church was a Norman castle.

In 1314, King Edward II of England invaded Scotland. Donal O'Neill, who was King of Ulster at that time, sent a contingent of archers over to help the Scottish forces. The Scots were under the command of Robert Bruce. The Irish soldiers contributed greatly to the victory at Bannockburn. Chaucer in writing about that battle stated:

> To Albion Scots we ne'er would yield;
> The Irish bowmen won the field.

Donal O'Neill, after the success of Bannockburn, organized a confederacy of Irish chiefs and invited Edward Bruce, Robert's brother, to come over to Ireland and join with this confederation to deliver Ireland from her oppressors. Bruce accepted and with six thousand men, landed at Glenarm in County Antrim. The combined forces had soon captured all of Ulster, with the exception of Carrickfergus. Bruce was elected king of Ireland and was crowned in Dundalk in 1315 amid great celebrations. In 1316, Bruce's army attacked the Norman castle in Naas and won another great battle. The English amalgamated all of their forces under Birmingham and De Burgh and finally defeated Bruce's army at Faughart in County Louth on 14 October 1319. Edward Bruce was slain in that battle.

During the Middle Ages, there were several monasteries here in Naas. Alas, not a stone of any of them remains standing.

A view of Powerscourt's stunning four-hundred-foot waterfall. (photo provided by the Irish Tourist Board)

Powerscourt, County Wicklow

In the delightful, old-worldly village of Enniskerry, in County Wicklow, is the entrance to the magnificent Powerscourt Estate. The Georgian mansion, designed by Richard Cassels in 1731, was altered and enlarged in the nineteenth century. In 1974, it was badly damaged by fire. The site on which the house stands was an Anglo-Norman stronghold built by the de La Poer family. There is a growing hope that the mansion will be restored in the near future.

The Powerscourt Estate is noted for its exquisite gardens. It is regarded as one of the great garden complexes of Europe. The gardens were begun in 1745 and finished in 1767. They include Japanese, Italian and English sections. The top terrace is eight hundred feet long. It affords a wonderful view of Sugarloaf Mountain, viewed across the Triton Pool. The pool has a sixty-foot fountain and is guarded by the winged horses Fame and

Victory. There is not a more beautiful or tranquil place in Ireland. A day spent here is a day of complete spiritual peace.

Deer Park Glen is part of the estate. It is horseshoe shaped and leads to a four-hundred-foot waterfall, where the Dargle River plunges over a precipice to form one of the highest waterfalls in these islands.

Powerscourt . . . truly breath-taking!

16

DUBLIN, ME JEWEL

Dublin's O'Connell Bridge and Westmoreland Street. (photo provided by the Irish Tourist Board)

Dublin

This is Dublin, capital city of Ireland. At first glance she is elegant, regal, haughty, intellectual, cosmopolitan and, undoubtedly, in the front rank of European capitals. When you get to know her even slightly, it becomes obvious, very quickly, that she can loose her girdle, put on comfortable shoes and relax completely. While retaining her elegance she becomes a voluminous talker, big-hearted, warm, humourous, even gossipy; she whispers secrets; looks on the ways of the world with benevolence, tolerance and wit. She's never in a hurry. For her, time is made to be enjoyed. She's colourful, rollicking, loquacious; very opinionated on every conceivable subject under the sun; thinks that anyone not from Dublin is underprivileged, and immediately takes them to her heart to console them with the warmest of welcomes.

She's proud of herself and of all her sons and daughters, including her adopted children. The conversations in her streets, her shops, her pubs, her buses and trains are stimulating, funny, stunning, brilliant, wise and many times downright fabrications, but never dull. They have reached legendary proportions. The unwritten flow of poetry continues day after day in an endless river of creative conversation. Anna Livia Plurabelle keeps ever flowing. Above all else, Dublin is proud of her heritage.

Dublin was founded by the Vikings in the ninth century and just a few years ago celebrated her thousandth anniversary. The Irish name *Baile Atha Cliath* means "The Town of the Ford of the Hurdles." The River Liffey divides the city and flows into Dublin Bay. Very few medieval buildings still stand, but wonderful architecture can be found all over the city. Graceful Georgian squares like Merrion Square and Parnell Square lend charm to this elegant, friendly city.

The Liffey is spanned by numerous bridges, the best known being O'Connell Bridge. It was named for Dan O'Connell, the champion of Catholic emancipation, who was nicknamed "The Liberator." The Ha'penny Bridge is so called because of the half penny toll that had to be paid to cross.

St. Stephen's Green, a beautiful park in the heart of the city is reputed to be the largest city square in Europe.

The open-air markets in Moore Street have all the ambiance of a Mardi Gras every day.

Dublin has a long and celebrated theatrical history. The

Abbey Theatre, which was founded in 1904, is world famous. It was nursed in its infancy by the great literary renaissance of the early twentieth century, spearheaded by Yeats, Synge and Lady Gregory. Playwrights like Sean O'Casey were nurtured here and a glorious list of world-class actors like the Fay brothers, Sarah Allgood, Barry Fitzgerald and for me, personally, the greatest of them all, F. J. McCormick.

Many of today's stage stars worked at the Abbey. They range from the late veterans Cyril Cusack and Siobhan McKenna to Anna Manahan, Donal McCann, John Kavanagh and a long list of notables. Other theatres, like The Gate, which gave Ireland the storied collaboration of Hilton Edwards and Michael MacLiammor, The Gaiety, The Olympia and the beloved Theatre Royal which was knocked down for what was termed progress, have all added to the legend. There is a host of other smaller companies. They are vibrant and hard-working and have produced many important, exciting dramatic events and moments for this very theatrical city.

The National Museum in Kildare Street is home to most of the nation's treasures. Here we may enjoy the eighth-century Tara Brooch and the Ardagh Chalice from the same period; the eleventh-century Shrine of St. Patrick's Bell; the twelfth-century Cross of Cong and a very large collection of magnificent gold art treasures from various centuries B.C. and the early centuries A.D. Stone and Bronze Age treasures abound. In the musical instrument collection, they have the battered and beloved harp of Turlough O'Carolan, the seventeenth-century musical genius and poet.

Trinity College was founded by Elizabeth I in 1592. The oldest buildings in the complex are the Queen Anne buildings, called "The Rubrics," begun in 1700. Trinity houses around three thousand ancient manuscripts. These include the magnificent *Book of Kells,* the *Book of Durrow,* the *Book of Armagh,* the *Book of Leinster* and the *Yellow Book of Lecan.* It has a first folio Shakespeare and is home to Brian Boru's harp. Brian Boru was the king of Ireland in the early eleventh century. He was killed in his tent by a wandering enemy after he had defeated the Vikings at the very significant Battle of Clontarf in Dublin in 1014.

An interesting point in the port below the Customs House is that it was partly designed by Captain Bligh who later won fame (or was it infamy?) on the good ship *The Bounty.*

St. Michan's Church was built in 1095. It is situated in the old Norse district known as Ostmantown. The building, which was restored in the nineteenth century, was built in yellow limestone. Its moisture-absorbing properties preserve bodies in the crypt where they become mummified. Visitors may see some of the mummified bodies. John and Henry Shears, who were executed for their part in the rebellion of 1798, are interred here. Also here, supposedly, is the body of Robert Emmett, the twenty-three-year-old leader of a short-lived rebellion in 1803. The old organ, dated 1724 is the instrument on which Handel played the first performance of his "Messiah" here in Dublin in 1742.

Dublin's list of native men and women of letters and distinction is nearly endless. It includes, in no particular order, Dean Jonathan Swift whose works include *Gulliver's Travels.* He was Dean of St. Patrick's Cathedral. With his wife Stella, he is buried at the cathedral and the epitaph on his tombstone reads: "He lies where furious indignation can no longer rend his heart." Yeats described this as the greatest epitaph of all.

Michael Balfe, the composer, was a Dublin man, as were: Edmund Burke, the great orator; Thomas Moore, the poet and songwriter; the Duke of Wellington; Richard Brinsley Sheridan; Oscar Wilde; James Clarence Mangan, the poet; Wolfe Tone, the patriot; George Bernard Shaw; James Stephens; Sean O'Casey; Brendan Behan and, of course, James Joyce. Nearly any man or woman can point out Joycean places of interest. They know Davy Byrne's Pub in Duke Street and Mulligan's in Poolbeg Street. Most of them will know Olhausen's German Pig Butchery in Talbot Street. That is where Leopold Bloom bought a crubeen (pig's foot) on his way to the Monto, the Red Light district. Yeats was not born in Dublin, but lived here. So too did Patrick Kavanagh, the poet and other marvellous writers like Benedict Kiely and that comic genius Flann O'Brien, live here.

Phoenix Park, with its 1,752 acres, including a racecourse, is where the residence of the president of Ireland is located. The house is called Aras an Uachtarain. President Mary Robinson, the first female president of Ireland, after being inaugurated, introduced a lovely tradition at Aras an Uachtarain. She placed a light in one of the front windows as a perpetual beacon to welcome home anyone who has ever left Ireland. The residence of the United States ambassador to Ireland is also in Phoenix Park.

No visit to Dublin would be complete without an excursion to the Guinness Brewery. Arthur Guinness founded his brewery in 1759. It is the sole survivor of fifty-five breweries operating here in the nineteenth century. Guinness Stout is known in the most remote corners of the globe. Stout differs from ale in that stout is made from softer water. Guinness is not made from River Liffey water as is widely believed. Roast barley from the farms of Ireland give it its distinct colour and flavour. Guinness advertising is instantly recognizable and quite famous, too. Many copywriters have contributed to the advertising down the years. Amongst them is British mystery writer Dorothy L. Sayers, creator of the Lord Peter Wimsey stories. She is credited with writing the advertising copy that went with a cartoon drawing of a black parrot-like bird, with a cream-coloured bill, called a Toucan. The copy read:

> If he can say as you can,
> Guinness is good for you,
> How grand to be a toucan,
> Just think what toucan do.

Dublin is a jewel, as Sean O'Casey might have written. It's very hard to leave her. Savor her many delights just once, and the longing will always remain to come back again and again. Don't deny that longing.

I have had many memorable moments in my career; performing for President Kennedy in Washington, D.C.; every one of the numerous sold-out performances in Carnegie Hall; playing to forty thousand people on Boston Common; singing to full houses in the Royal Albert Hall in London; the wonderful Newport Folk Festivals; touring Australia and New Zealand for the first time; performing in the Maritimes in Eastern Canada at any time; the list goes on and on. For me, arguably, the most moving and exciting moment in my career was when the Clancy Brothers and I did the opening concert of our first tour of Ireland at the Olympia Theatre in Dublin in 1962.

The venerable Ciaran Mac Mathuna, long considered an institution in Irish music, especially in broadcasting, had come to the United States to collect music from the many fine fiddlers, flute players, pipers, and accordianists who were working very hard to keep traditional music alive in all the large cities of the United States. Armed with his trusty tape recorder and his many contacts in the Irish musical communities, he was spending night after night in various locations recording hundreds of tunes for his radio programmes and indeed for posterity. In every house and every apartment he visited, he noticed that, inevitably, beside the phonograph in the living room there were LP recordings with four fellows in Aran sweaters on the covers. Having had his curiosity aroused, he returned to Ireland with an armful of these seemingly popular recordings.

Ciaran started playing the records on Radio Eireann and very soon they were being played on all the various programmes and went soaring sky-high in popularity. The entire population of the country had rediscovered their own songs and music. Suddenly realizing that their own culture was as good as, and, in some cases, better than most of what they had been hearing on the radio, the nation's enthusiasm knew no bounds.

With a couple of his friends who were promoters, and encouraged by journalists like Joe Kennedy, Ciaran Mac Mathuna invited the Clancy Brothers and Tommy Makem to do a concert tour of Ireland.

Not knowing the extent of the popularity of our songs in Ireland, we approached the first concert at the Olympia Theatre in Dublin a little tentatively. This was our first group appearance in our native land. Also, this was the first time that an entire concert programme was being performed by one act, as far as we knew. We were bringing their own songs to the people and we didn't know how they would react to them.

Even before the concert started we realised that all our fears were groundless. The theatre was jammed full, even the aisles, and if I'm not mistaken, there were some people sitting on the stage. Someone told us that there was a large crowd of people who couldn't get in and that they refused to leave the street outside. The four of us went to a first-floor window, opened it, and there, sure enough was a large crowd standing in the rain, cheering and waving to us. Someone shouted up "Give us a bar of a song," so we obliged with four or five songs which the rain-soaked crowd roared lustily along with us and added many accompanying cheers.

The atmosphere inside the theatre was electrically charged and from the first note of the first song to the last note of "The Parting Glass," the songs thundered from the collective voice of the enthusiastic crowd, shaking the beautiful old theatre to its very foundations.

It was a wild, glorious, emotionally moving night. No one wanted to leave the theatre, least of all the four of us. Dublin had embraced us with all the enormous warmth for which she is so famous. We were home!

Young Land, Ancient Land

Roam her highways and byways,
Trudge her mountain tracks,
Wander her country loanins,*
Her boggy paths and heathery bracken.
Talk and laugh and sing

*Loanin is an Ulster colloquialism for a lane.

With young people, who are ancient,
Shaped by teeming millennia
Of scholar, saint and sinner,
Of artist, poet and warrior;
By hands that have carved their story
On stone, on bronze, on gold,
On hearts and hidden memory;
Shaped too, by harps
That have strewn their songs
On the winds of Erin.

Dance modern streets
With ancient people, who are young,
Who carve their story, still,
On gold and bronze and stone;
Who lift the harps again,
And strew their songs
On the winds of the world.
Let your soul soar
Through a land
Of legend, of mystery,
Of everlasting beauty.

Put on your dancing shoes,
We'll dance in Ireland.

—TOMMY MAKEM

INDEX

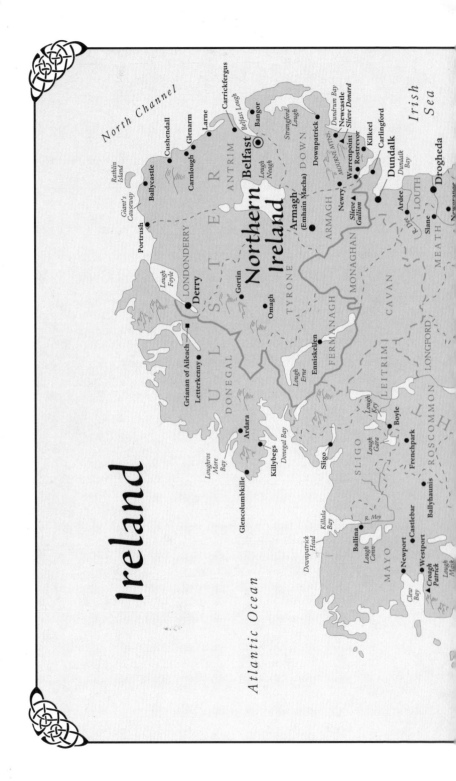